# Walks in
# The Peak District

Guide to 20 walks all over 5 miles

Published by Collins
*An imprint of* HarperCollins Publishers
Westerhill Road
Bishopbriggs
Glasgow G64 2QT

www.harpercollins.co.uk

First edition 2012

Mapping on the inner front cover and all
walking planning maps generated from
Collins Bartholomew digital databases

This product uses map data licensed from
Ordnance Survey ® with the permission of the
Controller of Her Majesty's Stationery Office.
© Crown copyright. Licence number 399302

Printed in China

ISBN  978 0 00 746455 5

email: collinsmaps@harpercollins.co.uk

Follow us on twitter 🐦 @CollinsMaps

# Contents

## ▶ Walks

# Introduction

Walking in the Peak District

### Walking in the Peak District

When walking in the Peak District you can encounter some quite different types of terrain. Probably the easiest walking of all is on the limestone plateau where stone stiles and green lanes indicate the way. In the dales, paths wander through shady woodland and follow bubbling trout rivers. In the north, the unpredictable weather makes navigation across the trackless moors quite difficult. Gritstone edges above the Derwent, or the lower heather moors, are more straightforward and the footpaths are easier to follow.

Walking is a pastime which can fulfil the needs of everyone. You can adapt it to suit your own preferences and it is one of the healthiest of activities. This book is aimed at walkers who prefer a slightly longer venture into the hills and countryside than in Collins' Short Walks in the Peak District. All walks are however, well within the reach of anyone with a reasonable level of fitness and it doesn't take long to find yourself in some lovely countryside. The walks are between five and nine miles and should easily be completed in two to five hours. Walking can be anything from an individual pastime to a family stroll, or maybe a group of friends enjoying the fresh air and open spaces of our countryside. There is no need for walking to be competitive and, to get the most from a walk, it shouldn't be regarded simply as a means of covering a given distance in the shortest possible time.

### What is the Peak District?

The title 'Peak District' is something of a misnomer. The name 'Peak', in fact, refers to a tribe who lived in the area in ancient times. In the year 924, a cleric writing about the hills and dales of what is now North Derbyshire, referred to the inhabitants as living in 'Peaclond' and the name seems to have stuck.

There are really two Peak Districts – Dark and White. The two areas are so completely different that, when standing on the breezy limestone plateau of the White Peak, it is hard to imagine that the untamed wilderness of

Bleaklow and Kinder Scout are not far away. Broadly speaking, the Peak District can be sub-divided into six distinct areas;

- The most northerly is the wildest and covers the moors above Saddleworth and the Longdendale Valley with the huge spread of Bleaklow filling the space between Longdendale and the Snake Pass.

- Kinder Scout is a vast boggy plateau bordered to its south by Edale and the graceful sweep of the Mam Tor - Rushup Edge Ridge.

- To the east, rising above the Derwent Valley, there is a long escarpment which is clearly defined by a series of gritstone edges backed by heather moorland.

- In the west, gritstone crags range from The Roaches above Leek to Windgather Rocks and Castle Naze on the northern limits. High open moors offer miles of lesser known walking. Tranquil wooded valleys cutting the western moors are excellent places to walk on hot summer days.

- Limestone makes its most northerly appearance in dramatic cliffs and knolls above Castleton, a place of caves and ancient lead mines. South of Castleton are some of the highest villages in the White Peak. They can expect to be cut off by deep snow for several days during most winters.

- The limestone plateau to the southwest of the A6 is incised by deep valleys and is judged by many to be the prettiest part of the Peak. It is certainly a zone of contrasts where the lush pastures of the rolling uplands have been grazed by cattle since time immemorial. Rivers run pure and clear and they are full of lively trout.

People came early to the Peak. Settling first on the treeless limestone plateau, they left mysterious mounds and stone circles. The circle at Arbor Low between Hartington and Youlgreave was probably the most important. Certainly its surrounding earthworks indicate its significance. Arbor Low is unique as the stones lie flat, unlike the more familiar uprights associated with other circles.

Peak District landscape, near Bakewell

During the Middle Ages, most of the lands were owned by various monasteries. They continued to exploit the lead resources, which was then very much in demand both as a roofing material and for constructing pipes to supply water into a growing number of monastic establishments. The monks opened large tracts of arable grazing and produced wool to clothe an expanding population. Farms which today have the word Grange as part of their name, were owned by rich monasteries until their dissolution by Henry VIII.

Great houses have been built in the Peak. Some are well known, like Chatsworth with its parkland, which was landscaped by Capability Brown, or Haddon Hall – a uniquely preserved medieval country house. There are also many lesser-known stately homes throughout the district which are just as interesting. Most are in private hands, like Tissington Hall which has been owned by the same family for generations. Hartington Hall, a fine example of a Jacobean yeoman's house is now a youth hostel as is Ham Hall which is an early Victorian mansion preserved by the National Trust.

Visitors to the Peak can buy jewellery made from Blue John, a semi precious stone found only beneath Treak Cliff, near Castleton. Another Peak novelty is the Bakewell Pudding (never call it a tart!). This delicacy was first made accidentally by a 19th century cook working in the Rutland Arms Hotel. Very fine.

Famous writers have penned the virtues of the Peak but none has better links than Izaak Walton (author of 'The Compleat Angler' published in 1653), who fished The Dove with the poet Charles Cotton.

Industry has always made its mark. Pack horse, or 'jaggers' tracks can still be followed on foot over the northern moors. Saltways crossed the southern dales. Water-powered mills in the early part of the Industrial Revolution brought textile production to the dales. Fluorspar, a nuisance to the early lead miners, is now extracted by open cast mining and used as a flux in steel making and as the basis for a number of chemicals.

Today, without any doubt, it is quarrying which makes the greatest industrial impact on the face of the Peak District. Limestone, suitable either as road aggregates or for cement making, is often only found in scenically attractive areas and, as a result, the quarries can make an ugly scar on the landscape unless they are carefully monitored.

## Geology
The rocks which made the foundations of the Peak District were laid down millions of years ago in a warm sea. Miriads of sea creatures living on the slimy bottom built up the great depth of limestone. Tropical lagoons were fringed by coral reefs which, through time, have become the rounded hills of Thorpe Cloud, Parkhouse and Chrome Hills in Dovedale. Minor volcanic activity took place during this time. The best

examples of this can be found in the small outcrops of basalt near Castleton and in the dolerite quarry which is part of the Tideswell Dale Nature Trail. Lead found its way in gaseous form, through minute cracks in the underlying rocks, laying down the basis of what became a major industry thousands of centuries later. Copper was also deposited in this way, occurring beneath Ecton Hill in the Manifold valley.

A mighty river delta flooded into the tropical sea, depositing mud and sand which consolidated to make the gritstones of the Dark Peak and the shales of Mam Tor.

Gradually, the layers of limestone and gritstone bulged from pressures deep within the earth and the middle and edges split. Ice action later honed the land into the beginning of the Peak District's rocky pattern. At the end of the Ice Age, huge volumes of melt water continued this shaping. The water carved caverns within the limestone of Castleton and Matlock as well as the pot holes of Eldon and it also created the beautiful dales. The land tilted as it buckled to give west facing gritstone outcrops on both sides of the Peak.

## Wildlife in the Peak District

Grouse spend their hardy lives on the high moors of the Dark Peak feeding on the tender shoots of young heather. Their tough existence is rudely shattered for four months of every year beginning on the 'Glorious Twelfth of August'. Not so common, and regrettably often shot by mistake, are their cousins the black grouse. Birds of prey have their chosen areas and many migrants, some quite rare, visit quieter sanctuaries on the moors from time to time. Mountain hares are common despite an inability to quickly shed their winter camouflage once the snows have gone. Foxes live a frugal life, mainly dependent upon voles and other small creatures. Plant life on the acid moors has to be tough to combat the extreme weather conditions. Heathers, coarse grass and berry plants such as bilberry, cloudberry and crowberry manage to survive in this harsh environment.

The limestone plateau is much more gentle. It is mainly given over to grazing and masses of colourful flowers still fill the hayfields and road verges. Scabious, meadow cranesbill and other plants, which were once scarce, have made a recent comeback in fields where far-sighted farmers have moved back to natural and cheaper methods of fertilising the land. Plant, and to a certain extent animal life, in the dales depend on the underlying strata. The Upper Derwent and its tributaries flow mostly through shale and gritstone. Forests planted around the Derwent Reservoirs are a major feature and offer homes to woodland birds and a few deer as well as the smaller carnivorous animals. In the limestone dales, trees were once cut down for fuel but they are plentiful today and, in some instances, they are crowding other plant life. In Dovedale, a courageous scheme has removed much of the invasive woodland to recreate more open vistas. Plant life on the craggy scree-covered hillsides is mostly dwarf and with an almost alpine quality. But the dales are best known for their trout streams. Not only do game fish breed in their clear waters, but crayfish, a crustacean which needs pure water, is found beneath the rocks of most of the rivers in the dales.

## The Peak District National Park

The Peak District National Park was designated in 1951 and extends over 542 square miles (1404 sq.km). Divided into two uniquely different zones, with wild gritstone moors to the north and gentler limestone uplands and dales to the south, it is surrounded by millions of people living in the industrial areas of England. Due to the advent of motorways the Peak is accessible to the bulk of the population in under two hours. The Peak District was the first National Park and is the most visited.

Administration of the park is controlled by a committee composed, on a proportional basis of representatives of the surrounding County, City, District and Borough Councils as well as members appointed by the Secretary of State for the Environment.

One of the statutory functions of a Park Authority is the appointment of full-time and voluntary Park Rangers. These are people with particular knowledge of some aspects of the local environment who are available

to give help and advice to visitors. Other functions of the Ranger Service include giving assistance to local farmers in such matters as rebuilding damaged walls to prevent stock from straying and leading guided walks from one of the Information Centres. Permanent Information Centres open all year are based at Edale, Castleton, Bakewell and Fairholmes. There are other information centres throughout the National Park.

One of the first tasks the Peak District National Park set itself after its formation in 1951 was to negotiate access agreements. These were not always straightforward but, by careful and diplomatic negotiation, agreements have been reached with farmers and landowners giving free access to most of the high moors of the Dark Peak. Large parts of moorland, including Kinder Scout, are open to unrestricted walking and rock climbing apart from a few days in summer when sections of the moors are closed for grouse shooting. Notices are published locally showing the dates when the moors are closed and there are also signposts giving dates at access points to the moors.

Losehill Hall National Park Learning and Environmental Conference Centre is a converted Victorian mansion which is set in spaciously wooded grounds to the south of Lose Hill. Residential and day courses are held on a wide variety of topics ranging from environmental studies, archaeology and the National Park and the pressures it faces, to hill walking, cycling, caving and more specialised subjects.

# Walking tips & guidance

## Safety
As with all other outdoor activities, walking is safe provided a few simple common sense rules are followed:

- Make sure you are fit enough to complete the walk;

- Always try to let others know where you intend going, especially if you are walking alone;

- Be clothed adequately for the weather and always wear suitable footwear;

- Always allow plenty of time for the walk, especially if it is longer or harder than you have done before;

- Whatever the distance you plan to walk, always allow plenty of daylight hours unless you are absolutely certain of the route;

- If mist or bad weather come on unexpectedly, do not panic but instead try to remember the last certain feature which you have passed (road, farm, wood, etc.). Then work out your route from that point on the map but be sure of your route before continuing;

- Do not dislodge stones on the high edges: there may be climbers or other walkers on the lower crags and slopes;

- Unfortunately, accidents can happen even on the easiest of walks. If this should be the case and you need the help of others, make sure that the injured person is safe in a place where no further injury is likely to occur. For example, the injured person should not be left on a steep hillside or in danger from falling rocks. If you have a mobile phone and there is a signal, call for assistance. If, however, you are unable to contact help by mobile and you cannot leave anyone with the injured person, and even if they are conscious, try to leave a written note explaining their injuries and whatever you have done in the way of first aid treatment. Make sure you know exactly where you left them and then go to find assistance. Make your way to a telephone, dial 999 and ask for the police or mountain rescue. Unless the accident has happened within easy access of a road, it is the responsibility of the police to arrange evacuation. Always give accurate directions on how to find the casualty and, if possible, give an indication of the injuries involved;

- When walking in open country, learn to keep an eye on the immediate foreground while you admire the scenery or plan the route ahead. This may sound difficult but will enhance your walking experience;

- It's best to walk at a steady pace, always on the flat of the feet as this is less tiring. Try not to walk directly up or downhill. A zigzag route is a more comfortable way of negotiating a slope. Running directly downhill is a major cause of erosion on popular hillsides;

- When walking along a country road, walk on the right, facing the traffic. The exception to this rule is, when approaching a blind bend, the walker should cross over to the left and so have a clear view and also be seen in both directions;

- Finally, always park your car where it will not cause inconvenience to other road users or prevent a farmer from gaining access to his fields. Take any valuables with you or lock them out of sight in the car.

## Equipment

Equipment, including clothing, footwear and rucksacks, is essentially a personal thing and depends on several factors, such as the type of activity planned, the time of year, and weather likely to be encountered.

All too often, a novice walker will spend money on a fashionable jacket but will skimp when it comes to buying footwear or a comfortable rucksack. Blistered and tired feet quickly remove all enjoyment from even the most exciting walk and a poorly balanced rucksack will soon feel as though you are carrying a ton of bricks. Well designed equipment is not only more comfortable but, being better made, it is longer lasting.

Clothing should be adequate for the day. In summer, remember to protect your head and neck, which are particularly vulnerable in a strong sun and use sun screen. Wear light woollen socks and lightweight boots or strong shoes. A spare pullover and waterproofs carried in the rucksack should, however, always be there in case you need them.

Winter wear is a much more serious affair. Remember that once the body starts to lose heat, it becomes much less efficient. Jeans are particularly unsuitable for winter wear and can sometimes even be downright dangerous.

Waterproof clothing is an area where it pays to buy the best you can afford. Make sure that the jacket is loose-fitting, windproof and has a generous hood. Waterproof overtrousers will not only offer complete protection in the rain but they are also windproof. Do not be misled by flimsy nylon 'showerproof' items. Remember, too, that garments made from rubberised or plastic material are heavy to carry and wear and they trap body condensation. Your rucksack should have wide, padded carrying straps for comfort.

It is important to wear boots that fit well or shoes with a good moulded sole – blisters can ruin any walk! Woollen socks are much more comfortable than any other fibre. Your clothes should be comfortable and not likely to catch on twigs and bushes.

It is important to carry a compass, preferably one of the 'Silva' type as well as this guide. A smaller scale map covering a wider area can add to the enjoyment of a walk. Binoculars are not essential but are very useful for spotting distant stiles and give added interest to viewpoints and wildlife. Although none of the walks in this guide venture too far from civilisation, on a hot day even the shortest of walks can lead to dehydration so a bottle of water is advisable.

Finally, a small first aid kit is an invaluable help in coping with cuts and other small injuries.

## Public Rights of Way

In 1949, the National Parks and Access to the Countryside Act tidied up the law covering rights of way. Following public consultation, maps were drawn up by the Countryside Authorities of England and Wales to show all the rights of way. Copies of these maps are available for public inspection and are invaluable when trying to resolve doubts over little-used footpaths. Once on the map, the right of way is irrefutable.

Right of way means that anyone may walk freely on a defined footpath or ride a horse or pedal cycle along a public bridleway. No one may interfere with this right and the walker is within his rights if he removes any obstruction along the route, provided that he has not set out purposely with the intention of removing that obstruction. All obstructions should be reported to the local Highways Authority.

In England and Wales rights of way fall into three main categories:

- Public Footpaths – for walkers only;

- Bridleways – for passage on foot, horseback, or bicycle;

- Byways – for all the above and for motorized vehicles

Free access to footpaths and bridleways does mean that certain guidelines should be followed as a courtesy to those who live and work in the area. For example, you should only sit down to picnic where it does not interfere with other walkers or the landowner. All gates must be kept closed to prevent stock from straying and dogs must be kept under close control – usually this is interpreted as meaning that they should be kept on a leash. Motor vehicles must not be driven along a public footpath or bridleway without the landowner's consent.

A farmer can put a docile mature beef bull with a herd of cows or heifers, in a field crossed by a public footpath. Beef bulls such as Herefords (usually brown/red colour) are unlikely to be upset by passers by but dairy bulls, like the black and white Friesian, can be dangerous by nature. It is, therefore, illegal for a farmer to let a dairy bull roam loose in a field open to public access.

The Countryside and Rights of Way Act 2000 (the 'right to roam') allows access on foot to areas of legally defined 'open country' – mountain, moor, downland, heath and registered common land. You will find these areas shaded orange on the maps in this guide. It does not allow freedom to walk anywhere. It also increases protection for Sites of Special Scientific Interest, improves wildlife enforcement legislation and allows better management of Areas of Outstanding Natural Beauty.

Pennine Way

## The Country Code

The Country Code has been designed not as a set of hard and fast rules, although they do have the backing of the law, but as a statement of commonsense. The code is a gentle reminder of how to behave in the countryside. Walkers should walk with the intention of leaving the place exactly as it was before they arrived. There is a saying that a good walker 'leaves only footprints and takes only photographs', which really sums up the code perfectly.

Never walk more than two abreast on a footpath as you will erode more ground by causing an unnatural widening of paths. Also try to avoid the spread of trodden ground around a boggy area. Mud soon cleans off boots but plant life is slow to grow back once it has been worn away.

Have respect for everything in the countryside, be it those beautiful flowers found along the way or a farmer's gate which is difficult to close.

Stone walls were built at a time when labour costs were a fraction of those today and the special skills required to build or repair them have almost disappeared. Never climb over or onto stone walls; always use stiles and gates.

Dogs which chase sheep can cause them to lose their lambs and a farmer is within his rights if he shoots a dog which he believes is worrying his stock.

The moors and woodlands are often tinder dry in summer, so take care not to start a fire. A fire caused by something as simple as a discarded cigarette can burn for weeks, once it gets deep down into the underlying peat.

When walking across fields or enclosed land, make sure that you read the map carefully and avoid trespassing. As a rule, the line of a footpath or right of way, even when it is not clearly defined on the ground, can usually be followed by lining up stiles or gates.

Obviously flowers and plants encountered on a walk should not be taken but left for others passing to enjoy. To use the excuse 'I have only taken a few' is futile. If everyone only took a few the countryside would be devastated. If young wild animals are encountered they should be left well alone. For instance, if a fawn or a deer calf is discovered lying still in the grass it would be wrong to assume that it has been abandoned. Mothers hide their offspring while they go away to graze and browse and return to them at feeding time. If the animals are touched it could mean that they will be abandoned as the human scent might deter the mother from returning to her offspring. Similarly with baby birds, who have not yet mastered flight; they may appear to have been abandoned but often are being watched by their parents who might be waiting for a walker to pass on before coming out to give flight lesson two!

What appear to be harmful snakes should not be killed because firstly the 'snake' could be a slow worm, which looks like a snake but is really a harmless legless lizard, and second, even if it were an adder (they are quite common) it will escape if given the opportunity. Adders are part of the pattern of nature and should not be persecuted. They rarely bite unless they are handled; a foolish act, which is not uncommon; or trodden on, which is rare, as the snakes are usually basking in full view and are very quick to escape.

## Map reading

Some people find map reading so easy that they can open a map and immediately relate it to the area of countryside in which they are standing. To others, a map is as unintelligible as ancient Greek! A map is an accurate but flat picture of the three-dimensional features of the countryside. Features such as roads, streams, woodland and buildings are relatively easy to identify, either from their shape or position. Heights, on the other hand, can be difficult to interpret from the single dimension of a map. The Ordnance Survey 1:25,000 mapping used in this guide shows the contours at 5 metre intervals. Summits and spot heights are also shown.

The best way to estimate the angle of a slope, as shown on any map, is to remember that if the contour lines come close together then the slope is steep – the closer together the contours the steeper the slope.

Learn the symbols for features shown on the map and, when starting out on a walk, line up the map with one or more features, which are recognisable both from the map and on the ground. In this way, the map will be correctly positioned relative to the terrain. It should then only be necessary to look from the map towards the footpath or objective of your walk and then make for it! This process is also useful for determining your position at any time during the walk.

Let's take the skill of map reading one stage further: sometimes there are no easily recognisable features nearby: there may be the odd clump of trees and a building or two but none of them can be related exactly to the map. This is a frequent occurrence but there is a simple answer to the problem and this is where the use of a compass comes in. Simply place the map on the ground, or other flat surface, with the compass held gently above the map. Turn the map until the edge is parallel to the line of the compass needle, which should point to the top of the map. Lay the compass on the map and adjust the position of both, making sure that the compass needle still points to the top of the map and is parallel to the edge. By this method, the map is orientated in a north-south alignment. To find your position on the map, look out for prominent features and draw imaginary lines from them down on to the map. Your position is where these lines cross. This method of map reading takes a little practice before you can become proficient but it is worth the effort.

# How to use this book

This book contains route maps and descriptions for 20 walks, with areas of interest indicated by symbols (see below). For each walk particular points of interest are denoted by a number both in the text and on the map (where the number appears in a circle). In the text the route instructions are prefixed by a capital letter. We recommend that you read the whole description, including the fact box at the start of each walk, before setting out.

Route instruction
denoted by a capital
letter in the text

Point of interest
denoted by a number
in the text

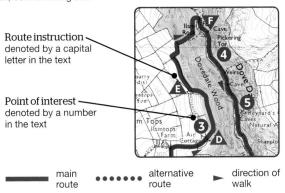

| ▬▬▬▬ | main route | •••••••• | alternative route | ► | direction of walk |

## Key to walk symbols
At the start of each walk there is a series of symbols that indicate particular areas of interest associated with the route.

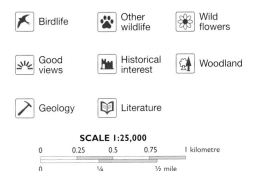

| | Birdlife | | Other wildlife | | Wild flowers |
| | Good views | | Historical interest | | Woodland |
| | Geology | | Literature | | |

**SCALE 1:25,000**

0    0.25    0.5    0.75    1 kilometre

0         ¼            ½ mile

Please note the scale for walk maps is 1:25,000 unless otherwise stated
North is always at the top of the page

> **The walk starts in Hayfield where travellers in time gone by sheltered before braving the high moors**

This is a valley stroll combined with a moorland ramble which offers wide-ranging views of Kinder Scout and its satellite moors. Well-defined paths allow it to be used in all but the severest weather conditions. The walk starts from the ancient stone-built village of Hayfield now bypassed by the busy A624 and where ample parking can usually be found in the Sett Valley Trail car park.

# Middle Moor & Little Hayfield

Packhorse road between Hayfield and Edale

## Plan your walk

Halifax  Wakefield
Rochdale  Huddersfield
Oldham  Barnsley
Ashton-under-Lyne
Manchester  Sheffield
Stockport
Macclesfield  Dronfield
Chesterfield
Buxton
Congleton  Matlock
Leek
Newcastle-under-Lyme  Ashbourne
Stoke-on-Trent
Derby
Stone  Uttoxeter

**DISTANCE:** 5 miles (8km)

**TIME:** 2½ hours

**START/END:** SK036869

**TERRAIN:** Moderate

**MAPS:**
OS Explorer OL 1;
OS Landranger 110

## Route instructions

**1** Travellers have set off from Hayfield for centuries. Originally at the start of a packhorse trail, it is now the hospitable venue for walkers climbing Kinder Scout.

**A** Go through the underpass into Hayfield village. Bear left past the church, then over the river, and follow the main street uphill and back under the main road.

**B** Walk past modern houses and turn right at the second street on the right to follow the tree-shaded side lane. Go past a group of cottages and cross a narrow bridge. Climb through sparse woodland, keeping on ahead at a signpost.

**C** Bear left uphill along the gravel path behind an old farmhouse.

**2** Look back at Hayfield in its sheltering hollow. Beyond it is Mount Famine and, to the right across the broad col, is Chinley Churn. To your left are the craggy ramparts of Kinder Scout.

**D** Cross a stile on the right to follow a level path through woodland.

**E** Turn right at the signpost and into a side valley. Turn right again along the surfaced lane as far as the main road. Turn left for about ¼ mile (400m). Because there is no path take great care as you go along the road,

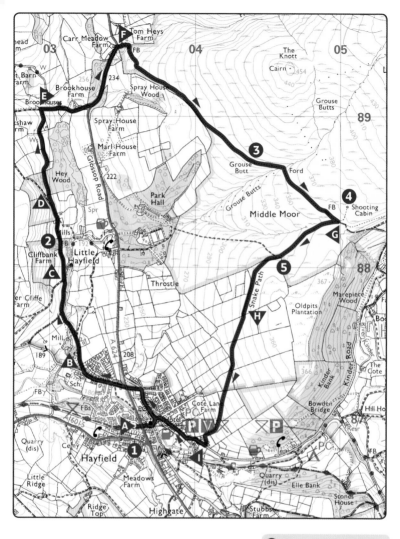

remembering to face the oncoming traffic.

**F** Opposite the group of cottages, turn right at the gate. Bear right to a footbridge, cross, and climb the winding moorland path.

**3** Ahead, Kinder Scout fills the far skyline, and to its right is the whaleback of Kinder Low; then Brown Knoll's long ridge leads to the twin summits of South Head and Mount Famine. Look right again to Chinley

# Middle Moor & Little Hayfield

Churn and the low rolling hills above the Sett Valley.

**4** The tiny cabin to your left is used by grouse shooters during the season. Beyond is the western escarpment of Kinder Scout.

**G** Turn right at the signpost to 'Hayfield' and walk along a sandy path meandering across the heather moor.

**5** The path on the left leads across the shoulder of Kinder to the Snake Pass.

**H** Go through a kissing gate and, after 100yds (90m), bear left on a descending path.

**I** Go down a flight of steps and turn right along the road into Hayfield. The car park and bus terminus are beyond the underpass behind the church.

Little Hayfield

This classic route is not a walk for the ill-prepared, be he or she improperly clothed for the prevailing weather conditions at 2000ft (600m), or generally unfit for what is an expedition across an open mountainside on the same latitude as Siberia. Remember that a warm sunny day in Hayfield can frequently turn to arctic-style weather on Kinder. Having given that warning, walkers who act sensibly will enjoy this exhilarating high-level walk through some of the most rugged countryside in the Peak District. The sense of achievement on looking back at the wild rocks around the Downfall will be just reward for the effort of the climb.

The walk starts from Bowden Bridge car park on the Kinder road from Hayfield. Leave the A624 and drive into the centre of the village; then follow a side road (Kinder Road) eastwards. If the car park is full, there is usually space along the road in the direction of Hayfield. Do not drive beyond Bowden Bridge as parking is restricted upstream of this point. Hayfield is served by several bus routes.

66 Within sight of Manchester, yet in winter the moorland around Kinder Downfall can be like the arctic 99

Looking out over Kinder Reservoir

# Kinder Downfall

**Edale Cross**

## Route instructions

**A** Follow the reservoir road uphill from the car park.

**1** A plaque on the quarry wall above the car park at Bowden Bridge commemorates the Mass Trespass on 24 April 1932 which led to five protesters being jailed for between two and six months. It has been argued that the trespass was unnecessary, but it and others which followed, certainly functioned as the catalyst which brought about post-war legislation to create National Parks and allow a greater freedom of access to the lonely places of England and Wales.

**B** Turn right by the metal gates and cross the bridge then left to follow the lane uphill past the farm.

**C** Turn left and go downhill across the valley. Turn right and go uphill along a rocky path above the reservoir buildings.

**D** Turn right along a path contouring to the left of the reservoir.

**2** Kinder Reservoir, one of Stockport's water supplies, is below. Two streams feed it from the east, the main one being the River Kinder which drains the boggy plateau of Kinder Scout. The other is William's Clough, named after a blacksmith whose now drowned smithy once stood at the bottom of this steep valley. His

## Plan your walk

**DISTANCE:** 8 miles (13km)

**TIME:** 4 hours

**START/END:** SK048869

**TERRAIN:** Strenuous; one climb of 1247ft (380m), boggy stretches, not suitable in mist or bad weather

**MAPS:**
OS Explorer OL 1;
OS Landranger 110

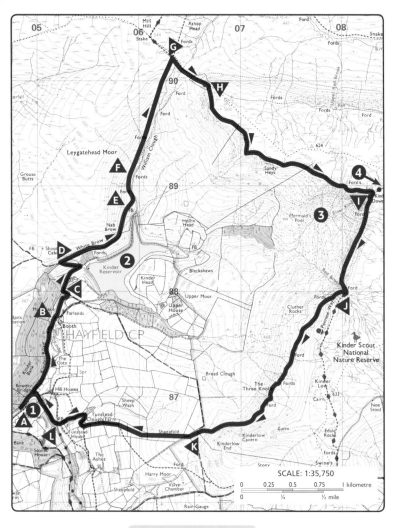

trade was mostly repairing
the shoes of pack-ponies
climbing the track over to
the Snake Pass. At one time,
this path was the only right of
way to the north of Kinder.

**E** Go down to the stream,
turn left, and follow it uphill,

crossing as indicated by
the steep path.

**F** Turn right on the broad
moorland saddle. Climb
steeply up to the escarpment.

**G** Follow the path to the
right around the rocky edge.

# Kinder Downfall

**H** Cross the rocky stream bed and begin to go downhill along the moorland path.

**3** Look down the rocky gorge towards the reservoir, and to the right of the stream there is a small pool where a mermaid is supposed to live. If you want to see her, come to the pool on a summer's night and, if you are lucky, you will be entertained by her charms, but beware as many have disappeared after a night by the Mermaid's Pool!

One of the possible origins of the name Kinder Scout, is from the Saxon *kyndwr scut* meaning 'water over the edge'. In summer an almost insignificant trickle flows over the steep jumble of crags known as the Downfall but, after heavy rain and with a strong westerly wind, a plume of water blows backwards and can be seen for miles. The crags are a popular climbing face, both for rock-climbers in summer and for devotees of ice climbing in winter. During particularly harsh winters, the ravine and surrounding rocks take on the appearance of a glacier.

**4** A ¼ mile (400m) diversion upstream from the Downfall along the sandy bed of the River Kinder leads to the twin outcropping crags of Kinder Gate Stones. The Pennine Way route once crossed Kinder at this point and many ambitions of prospective 'Wayfarers' foundered on the first day. Above and on all sides of the river, the boggy plateau of Kinder Scout waits to sap the strength of ill-prepared walkers. Deep, water-worn channels known as 'groughs' can lead the unwary astray.

Return to the Downfall to continue the walk along, then below, the western escarpment.

**I** Turn sharp right and cross a stream. Go to the right again across a depression and follow the path steeply downhill.

**J** Go ahead at the path crossing to follow a wall downhill towards a stile. Cross and continue to descend through improving farmland. Use kissing gates and stiles as necessary.

**K** Keep to the left of the house, then follow the waymarked path to the right, around the farm buildings. Join the access track and follow it downhill into the valley.

**L** Turn right along the valley bottom road; follow it back to the car park.

> **❝** This is a classic walk, a perfect introduction to the wilderness of Kinder Scout **❞**

Generations of walkers and climbers have approached Kinder Scout from Edale. On the moorland edge, gritstone rocks worn by wind and weather, are reminiscent of sculptures by Henry Moore.

The Pennine Way has its southern portal in Edale and many hopeful walkers have had to abandon their attempt right at the start because they were ill-prepared for the hazards of Kinder. Never attempt this walk in bad weather or mist.

# Grindsbrook Skyline

**walk 3**

The top of Grindsbrook,
Kinder Scout

## Route instructions

**A** From the car park below the railway station, follow the road through Edale village.

**1** Field Head, the Peak District National Park Information Centre. Call in to check the weather forecast and leave a note of your intended route.

**2** The Pennine Way long distance trail to Kirk Yetholm starts by the Nags Head Inn.

**B** Cross Grindsbrook by the narrow wooden footbridge. Follow the wide path for about 60yds (55m) to a stone barn. Beyond it turn right and walk uphill towards Heardman's Plantation.

**C** Climb the stile at the left of the plantation and walk uphill on a clear path to the open moors.

**D** Keep left at a path junction. Climb beneath the rocks of Ringing Roger, ascending steeply to the head of Golden Clough.

**3** Viewpoint. From the weather worn rocks of Nether Tor, look across the valley to Rushup Edge (right) and Mam Tor (left).

**E** A prominent cairn on the skyline marks the Kinder plateau. Turn left and follow the escarpment, taking care when crossing rocky streams.

**4** Viewpoint. Below is Grindsbrook. Deep tortuously

## Plan your walk

**DISTANCE:** 5½ miles (8.8km)

**TIME:** 2¾ hours

**START/END:** SK124852

**TERRAIN:** Strenuous; attempt only in fine weather; one 1210ft (369m) climb

**MAPS:**
OS Explorer OL 1;
OS Landranger 110

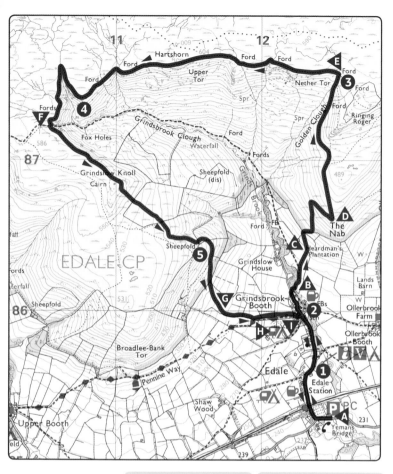

winding channels in the peat of Kinder are known as 'groughs'.

**F** At another large cairn, keep left following the moorland edge. Above rocky Fox Holes, aim for the prominent hump of Grindslow Knoll.

**5** Where the path enters a shallow groove below Grindslow Knoll, it follows the line of an old sledge track, made to drag peat from the moor.

**G** Climb the stile in the moorland boundary wall and walk down to a double line of old hawthorns.

**H** Turn left along a sunken track.

**I** A right turn in the village leads back to the car park.

# Grindsbrook Skyline

A waterfall in Grindsbrook

Here is a walk with contrasting views. Starting near the Ashopton viaduct, it leaves the reservoir by climbing steadily across the flank of Crook Hill along an ancient bridleway. This track carried people and goods between West Yorkshire and Cheshire, long before the Snake Road turnpike was built. The views from Crook Hill, especially those opposite, of the edges above the Derwent Valley, are most spectacular. Strange rock formations with fanciful names dot the eastern skyline and the eye is carried easily across the heights from scene to scene. Quiet forest glades lead down to the manmade lake of Ladybower where a quiet road is followed along its eastern shore, back to the busy A57.

During summer weekends and bank holidays, the road from Fairholmes to the dale head is free of all but essential motor traffic. A mini bus service carries pedestrians to various points along the road and a cycle hire scheme helps visitors enjoy the tranquility and beauty of this secluded valley.

66 On this walk the scenery changes almost by the yard, from the Lake District to the Scottish Highlands 99

# Ladybower

**Ladybower Reservoir**

## Route instructions

**A** The walk starts and finishes on the A57 close to the Ashopton viaduct. There is usually space to park in the scenic lay-by overlooking the reservoir.

**B** From the A57 walk along the Derwent Valley road for about 80yds (73m). Go through a narrow bridle gate on the left and climb diagonally, to the right, by a pathless route across three fields.

**C** At Crookhill Farm, go through two small bridleway gates next to a barn. Walk ahead, through the farmyard and left through a gate. Follow the cart track.

**D** Climb a ladder stile and cross a couple of improved fields. Leave by a bridleway gate to reach the open moor. Follow a grassy track marked by a series of posts and aim for the upper edge of the forestry plantation.

**1** Crook Hill viewpoint. To the east across the deep cleft of flooded Derwent Dale, the eastern skyline is marked by rocky outcrops, more in keeping with Dartmoor Tors. Most of the rocks are named but two, in particular, should be obvious from their shape, even at this distance: one is the 'Salt Cellar' and the other, the 'Coach & Horses' (marked 'Wheel Stones' on the OS map), is just like a 19th-century mail coach. Even though it is man-made and completely altered

## Plan your walk

**DISTANCE:** 6½ miles (10.5km)

**TIME:** 3¼ hours

**START/END:** SK195864

**TERRAIN:** Moderate; one 580ft (177m) climb

**MAPS:**
OS Explorer OL 1;
OS Landranger 110

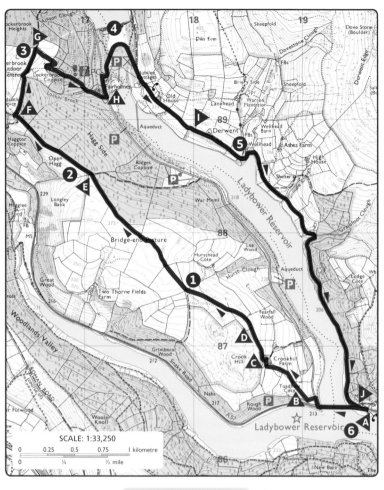

the appearance of the dale, Ladybower Reservoir makes an attractive contrast to the wild moors beyond. Westward from Crook Hill and across the Woodlands Valley arm of the reservoir, are the heights of Win Hill and Kinder Scout.

**E** Walk forwards at the footpath junction. Keep left of the forest boundary on a grassy track.

**2** Viewpoint. Kinder Scout's northern edges dominate the Ashop Valley and over the northern shoulder of Win Hill, Mam Tor's undulating ridge marks the boundary between the Dark and White Peak. To the north, the

# Ladybower

underlying rocks were laid down by an ancient river delta millions of years ago. The river in its turn buried the even older limestone, deposited by countless sea creatures in a tropical sea.

**F** Turn right along the track past Lockerbrook Farm.

**3** Viewpoint. From the farm look across Lockerbrook Plantation to Ladybower Reservoir and the Derwent Edges.

**G** About 200yds (183m) beyond the farm, turn right at the concessionary footpath sign and walk downhill across the field and into the forest. Follow yellow Forest Walk waymarks to Fairholmes.

**H** Cross the road and make your way through Fairholmes picnic site as far as the road below the Derwent Dam.

**4** Derwent Dam. When the reservoir is full, water cascades over the dam wall creating the largest waterfall in the Peak. The dam was used by members of the famous Dam Busters Squadron, when they were training for the wartime raids on the Möhne and Eder dams in the Ruhr. The same dam was used in the film portraying this courageous exploit.

**I** Follow the quiet road, as far as Grindle Clough. Beyond this point, the wide gravel track skirts the eastern shore of the reservoir.

**5** A plaque at the side of the Mill Brook tells the sad story of the lost village of Derwent. All that remains of this village is the re-erected war memorial on the roadside above the west shore of the reservoir. A graceful packhorse bridge, which was sited near the village, now crosses the River Derwent at Slippery Stones almost at the head of the valley.

**6** There is another drowned village below this point. This was Ashopton, once reached by a steep tree-shrouded lane below the A57. It is hard to imagine, gazing out over millions of gallons of water, that the Derwent flowed past Ashopton on its way south through a deep rocky valley. All that tranquility ended in 1943, when the sluices were shut and water drowned an idyllic valley with its farms and villages.

**J** Join the main road and turn left or right, depending upon where you have parked the car.

> **The honey pot of Castleton is soon left behind for this exhilarating high level tramp**

The skyline immediately to the north of Castleton is a rugged ridge with three distinct summits along its length. The highest point is Mam Tor on your left where Iron Age people built a refuge surrounded by a complex of defensive ridges. Castleton is popular with thousands of visitors who come each year to visit its caves, climb the steep slope of the castle or simply to enjoy the local scenery. This walk leaves Castleton by an almost hidden route and climbs to the limestone uplands along the bed of a collapsed cave. Mam Tor dramatically marks the change from limestone to the gritstone and shales of the Dark Peak. To the west and out of sight, the Great Ridge continues as Rushup Edge until it merges with the bleak moorland around Brown Knoll.

# The Great Ridge

**walk**

**5**

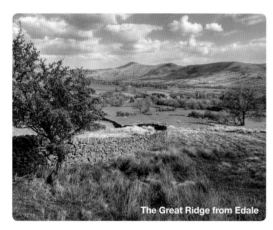

## Plan your walk

The Great Ridge from Edale

### Route instructions

**A** Turn right opposite the Bull's Head and follow the side street, bearing left and then right from the square.

**1** St Edmund's, Castleton's parish church, has a unique collection of bibles, including a Cranmer Bible of 1539 and a 'Breeches' Bible of 1611.

**B** Turn right, through a narrow opening between two rows of cottages. Go through a wicket gate and into Cave Dale.

**2** Castleton's castle was built in 1080 by William Peveril, son of the Conqueror, as a wooden stockade. The present stone keep dates from 1176, when it cost £135!

Castleton has two special events each year. The first is Garland Day held during the evening of 29th May to celebrate the restoration of the Monarchy. The second is Christmas when the village is decorated with dozens of illuminated Christmas trees.

**3** Beyond the iron gate at the top of the dale, there is a small outcrop of dull brown rock to the left. This is dolerite, a form of basalt left by an ancient volcano.

**C** Keep ahead at the track junction, following the shallow dry upland valley. Walk out to the grassy moor.

**4** The round shallow pond on the right of the

**DISTANCE:** 8½ miles (13.7km)

**TIME:** 3 hours

**START/END:** SK149829

**TERRAIN:** Strenuous; total ascent 1095ft (334m)

**MAPS:**
OS Explorer OL 1;
OS Landranger 110

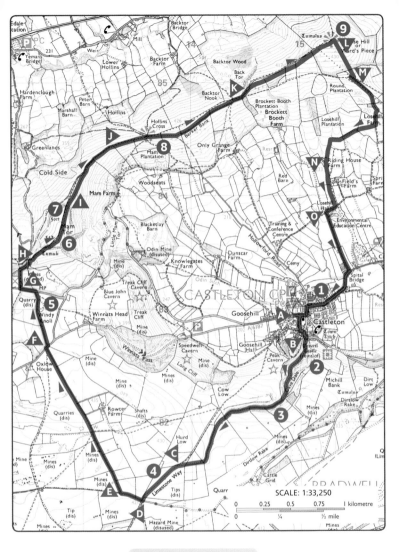

path is man-made, to hold rainwater on the dry limestone uplands.

**D** Climb a stile at the side of the gate. Turn right for about 150yds (137m) along a walled lane as far as another gate and stile.

**E** Climb the second stile and go to the right, following a lane, muddy in places, past Rowter Farm.

# The Great Ridge

**F** Cross the road and go through a stile on its opposite side. Follow a grassy path across the open field.

**5** Windy Knoll. The shallow depression has yielded fascinating relics of interest to both geologists and paleontologists. Bitumen exuding from the rocks hints that there was probably an infant oil field in the vicinity. In 1870 nearby Bone Cave yielded up the remains of a sabre toothed tiger and grisly bear.

**G** Cross the A625, diagonally left and then go through the car park.

**H** Climb the stile at the top of the car park, turn right and follow the road to Mam Nick. Turn right and climb the path to the top of Mam Tor.

**6** Mam Tor. The massive earthworks of an Iron Age fort can still be traced.

**7** The view from the summit takes in Kinder Scout and the Edale Valley to the north and, to the south east, you can see the Hope Valley and Castleton.

**I** Walk downhill away from the summit following the ruined wall towards the distinct col of Hollins Cross.

**J** Follow the ridge-top path, ahead and steeply uphill.

**8** Viewpoint. The entrance to the Winnats (Wind Gates) can be seen to the left of Treak Cliff.

**K** Go to the left across a stile, then immediately right to climb the shaley path up Back Tor. Continue along the ridge towards Lose Hill. Take care not to go too close to the shaley edge of Back Tor, especially in wet or windy weather.

**9** The hilltop of Lose Hill has one of the finest viewpoints in the Peak and a plaque indicates most of the distant features.

**L** Go to the right, downhill and over a stile and then beyond a prominent cairn begin to bear right, then left to pass a line of trees.

**M** Turn right at a signpost to Castleton and cross the stile by a second, to go downhill across fields as indicated by yellow waymarks.

**N** Do not go into the farmyard, but turn left to cross a stile and follow the path around the edge of the field above a shallow brook.

**O** Turn right along the lane past Losehill Hall and left at the junction. Go down to the road and turn right to return to Castleton.

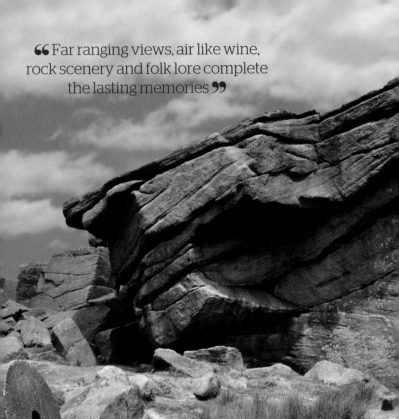

> **66** Far ranging views, air like wine, rock scenery and folk lore complete the lasting memories **99**

This is a walk steeped in romantic legend; Robin Hood's henchman, Little John, is reputed to be buried in Hathersage churchyard and the hero of Sherwood had an almost inaccessible refuge in a cave on Stanage Edge. The long, dramatic escarpment, where rock climbers can be seen practicing their skillful moves, has been scaled by climbers since the 1890s and has over 500 routes of varying technical difficulty. High Lees Hall, lying in a sunny sheltered valley below the rocks, featured in Charlotte Brönte's romantic novel, *Jane Eyre*.

Millstones littering the slopes below Stanage Edge were once in great demand for making wood pulp.

View from Stanage Edge,
Hathersage Moor

# Stanage Edge

Stanage Edge

## Route instructions

**A** Take the narrow path from the central car park. Go to the side of a farm house and cross the main road. Follow the lane opposite.

**B** Turn right, along the church path.

**1** Hathersage church. Little John's grave is opposite the main door. St Michael's church was built in the 14th and 15th centuries but it lies within the circular mound of a religion pre-dating Christianity.

**C** Turn left out of the lych gate and follow the lane. Go through a gate and keep to the right through the field, following the garden boundary. Go through a

kissing gate, then left along a farm lane.

**D** At the cattle grid, go right through a gate and follow the line of trees towards Toothill Farm. Bear right at the farm along a cart track.

**E** Turn left along the metalled road.

**F** Leave the road at the bend and follow a walled track. Climb steadily towards the open moors.

**2** Viewpoint looking uphill over the moors towards the rocky escarpment of Stanage Edge.

**G** Cross the stile in the wire boundary fence and

## Plan your walk

**DISTANCE:** 7 miles (11.3km)

**TIME:** 3½ hours

**START/END:** SK231813

**TERRAIN:** Moderate; 914ft (279m) climb

**MAPS:**
OS Explorer OL 1;
OS Landranger 110

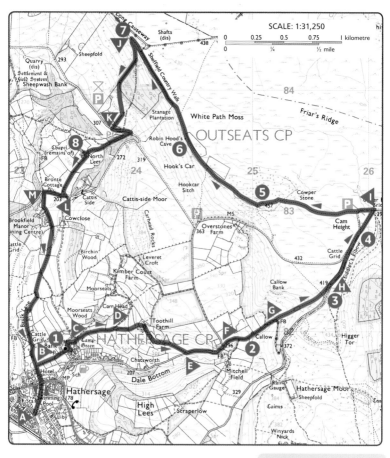

SCALE: 1:31,250

0    0.25    0.5    0.75    1 kilometre

0         ¼              ½ mile

walk uphill on the moorland footpath.

**3** Viewpoint. Hope Valley is to the far right with Eyam Moor to the left.

**H** Go left along the road, past the junction with Ladybower road.

**4** Viewpoint looking down to the enigmatic rocks of Carl Wark Fort on the right of a plantation of mixed conifers.

Burbage Rocks line the left upper rim of the valley.

**I** Turn left at the 'Open Country' sign. Aim towards the prominent Cowper Stone. Climb the outcrop on its left and follow a level path along the top of Stanage Edge.

**5** Viewpoint. This is one of the finest views in the Peak. The Derwent Edges reach towards the horizon and Rushup Edge, Win Hill,

# Stanage Edge

Kinder Scout and Bleaklow can be seen across the valley.

Southward, the view encompasses most of the uplands of the White Peak where clumps of trees on hilltops indicate ancient burial mounds. Millstones littering the foot of Stanage Edge were carved by stonemasons who then left them until required by the Scandinavian wood pulp industry. This trade died when longer-lasting steel rollers took over. The typical 'wheel' shape of these stones with flat outer rims, indicates their use as grindstones. Stones used for flour milling are usually bevelled.

**6** Robin Hood's Cave. This draughty opening in the rocks could well have been used by a local bandit in less settled times but it is unknown how this cave, and a well on nearby Longshaw Estate, came by the title.

**7** Viewpoint looking uphill towards the crags of Stanage Edge. The path at this point was once part of a pack horse way, an important link between Sheffield and Manchester.

**J** Turn left through a break in the crags and continue downhill on a flagged path to the mountain rescue post and public toilets.

**K** Turn right, on a wide track to North Lees Hall: go down its access drive.

**8** North Lees Hall. This three storied, semi-fortified manor house is something of a rarity so far south. Similar in purpose to the peel towers of the Scottish Borders, it offered protection to owners in the upper storeys and their animals on the ground floor.

North Lees and its estate, now cared for by the Peak National Park, for many generations was owned by the Eyre family, who were recorded amongst the bowmen at Agincourt.

Charlotte Brontë stayed at Hathersage Vicarage for three weeks in 1845 with her friend Ellen Massey and her novel *Jane Eyre* came as a result of that holiday. Many of the settings used in the story can be recognised as places around Hathersage. North Lees Hall is clearly identified as Thornfield Hall from which Jane fled.

**L** Turn right and walk downhill along the metalled road.

**M** Go through the gate on the left and follow the signposted field track. Join a farm access lane. Follow this into Hathersage.

The scenery has changed from that of a hundred years ago. Two reservoirs now flood the deep wooded valley and a secluded stately home, once surrounded by formal grounds, is a sad ruin.

> **The ridge marks the boundary between the Cheshire Plain and Peakland moors**

Shutlingsloe from Shining Tor

# Shining Tor & Errwood

Errwood Hall

## Plan your walk

Halifax   Wakefield
Rochdale
  Huddersfield
Oldham   Barnsley
Ashton-under-Lyne
Manchester
  Sheffield
Stockport
Macclesfield   Dronfield
Chesterfield
Buxton
Congleton
  Leek   Matlock
Newcastle-under-Lyme   Ashbourne
Stoke-on-Trent
  Derby
Stone   Uttoxeter

**DISTANCE:** 6½ miles (10.5km)

**TIME:** 3¼ hours

**START/END:** SK011746

**TERRAIN:** Moderate; total ascent 896ft (273m), boggy sections

**MAPS:**
OS Explorer OL 24;
OS Landranger 119

## Route instructions

**A** Follow the path uphill from the Nature Trail car park, through mixed woodland and rhododendron bushes, above the western arm of Errwood Reservoir.

**B** Cross the stream and climb along the old drive past the ruins of Errwood Hall. Beyond the hall, walk down to a second stream.

**1** Errwood Hall, once the home of the Grimshaw family, was built in 1830 and was the centre of a bustling community which existed until the late 1920s.

**C** Cross a tiny footbridge and climb to the left, above the stream. Climb over the moor towards the road.

**2** The tiny circular building to the left of the path is a shrine built in memory of Dolores de Bergrin, the Spanish governess of the Grimshaw children.

**D** Turn left and follow the road uphill to its summit.

**E** Leave the road by a signpost on the left and follow the moorland path uphill across Cats Tor to Shining Tor. Follow the boundary wall all the way.

**3** Viewpoint. On a clear day, the Cheshire Plain can be seen to the west: Alderley Edge is a final outlier of the Pennines and, beyond it, the Welsh Hills form the background. East, across the cleft of

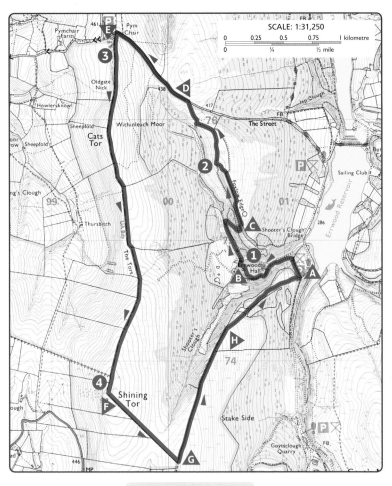

SCALE: 1:31,250

the Goyt Valley, is the wild moor of Combs Moss.

**4** Viewpoint. Macclesfield Forest, part of the Cheshire uplands, is dominated by the shapely peak of Shutlingsloe.

**F** Keep left at Shining Tor summit and cross the head waters of Shooter's Clough.

Keep to the left of the boundary wall.

**G** Cross the upper boundary wall and turn left along the old carriageway towards Errwood Hall.

**H** Bear right at the junction and follow the signposted path downhill back to the trail car park.

# Shining Tor & Errwood

Errwood Reservoir

> **Forest tracks lead to the summit of Cheshire's 'Matterhorn'**

Shutlingsloe is not the highest point of normally flat Cheshire but it certainly has the best shape of any hill on this the western boundary of the Peak District. We cross its rocky summit on this walk through the Cheshire Uplands.

Tegg's Nose, near
Macclesfield Forest

# Macclesfield Forest & Shutlingsloe

**Trentabank Reservoir**

## Route instructions

**A** From the lay-by car park, climb the short flight of steps and then cross a stile. Walk uphill along the broad path through mature pine forest.

**1** Trentabank Reservoir Nature Reserve. A plaque shows the commonest waterfowl on this attractive reservoir within Macclesfield Forest.

**B** Cross the stile in the upper forest boundary. Follow the signposted path out on to the open moor.

**C** Climb the stile and bear right over a stretch of boggy moor. Aim for the prominent summit of Shutlingsloe.

**2** Shutlingsloe, 1659ft (506m). A commemorative

plaque in the summit rocks gives the names of the prominent features seen from this vantage point. The valley, which the route next follows, is Wildboarclough and the ornamental lake opposite is within the grounds of Crag Hall, part of the estate of Lord Derby.

**D** Follow yellow arrows, steeply downhill through the summit rocks and across the lower moor. Cross the boundary wall by its stile and, still following waymarks, keep well to the right of the farm buildings. Turn right on the access drive and join the valley road conveniently close to the Crag Inn.

**E** Climb the flight of steps in the roadside wall at the

**DISTANCE:** 7 miles (11.3km)

**TIME:** 3½ hours

**START/END:** SJ962711

**TERRAIN:** Strenuous; one 759ft (231m) climb

**MAPS:**
OS Explorer OL 24;
OS Landranger 118

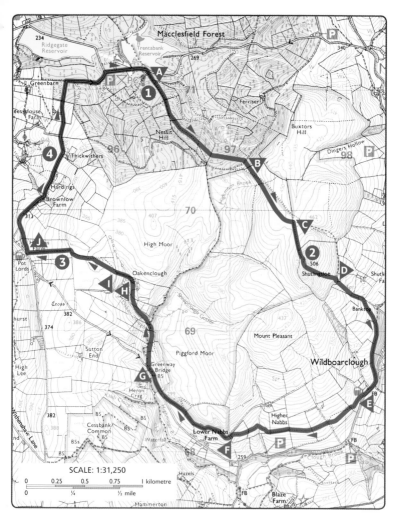

corner of the pub car park.
Follow the grassy path
above a clump of thorn
bushes. Cross a series of
pathless fields as indicated
by waymarks and stiles.

**F** Climb the stile and join
the farm lane near a sharp

bend. Turn left and follow
the lane as far as the road,
then turn right.

**G** Cross a stile on the right
by the side of Greenway
Bridge. Follow waymarks
upstream towards
Oakenclough. Keep left at

# Macclesfield Forest & Shutlingsloe

the junction with a lesser stream and then right of a small ruined barn.

**H** Keep below and left of both Oakenclough House and Farm. Cross the stream and climb to the access drive. Cross this and turn left uphill along an enclosed footpath.

**I** Bear right across rough moorland pasture and then left, downhill on a sunken track, aiming directly towards the Hanging Gate Inn.

**3** Viewpoint. Shutlingsloe is opposite, above Piggford Moor.

**J** Turn right at the pub, then right along the minor road, following it all the way back to Trentabank Reservoir. Keep right at all road junctions.

**4** Viewpoint. Tegg's Nose Country Park includes the overgrown quarries on the skyline. Below, the mature pines of Macclesfield Forest fill the valley and the scene is completed by Langley's twin reservoirs.

Shutlingsloe summit

> **❝** Wild moors and England's second highest pub are the main features of this walk **❞**

This is an easy-to-follow moorland walk from the second highest Inn in England (the highest is the Tan Hill Inn above Swaledale). Joined by Cumberland Clough, the walk continues along the pleasant Wildboarclough valley, in marked contrast with the wildness of the open moor. Parts of the moorland path can be boggy, especially after prolonged rain. Park opposite the Cat and Fiddle Inn at the highest point on the A537 Buxton to Macclesfield road.

# Cumberland Clough

View towards Wildboarclough

## Plan your walk

**DISTANCE:** 6 miles (9.5km)

**TIME:** 3 hours

**START/END:** SK001718

**TERRAIN:** Moderate; boggy sections

**MAPS:**
OS Explorer OL 24;
OS Landranger 118 & 119

## Route instructions

**A** Follow the moorland footpath directly opposite the Cat and Fiddle Inn.

**1** Look across the moor to the graceful heights of Shutlingsloe above the deep trough of Wildboarclough. The last wild boar is said to have been killed near here but, because there is no factual record, we must assume that, like all other similar folk stories, it is simply a myth.

**2** Look south over the Dane Valley to the Roaches escarpment and Hen Cloud. Beyond them are the rolling southern uplands of the Peak District.

**B** Turn right by the signpost

and go steeply down to the narrow valley.

**C** Join a track from the left and walk down the steadily improving path above a tree-lined stream.

**D** Go past farm buildings and down the access drive. Turn right along the valley road.

**E** Opposite the road junction, turn right and cross a bridge. Fork left and follow a stream-side farm lane uphill.

**F** Go through a farmyard and continue along the lane. Turn left to cross the stream and climb up to a barn. Bear right, along the footpath following a wall.

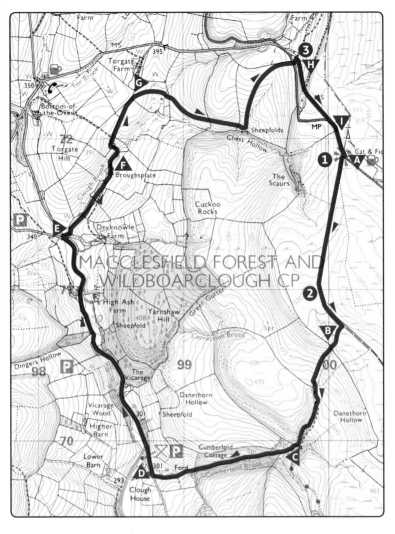

**G** With a second farm in view, go through a gateway and immediately turn right on to a concessionary path. Follow the waymarked path over a boggy side stream and contour round and into a narrow valley, crossing stiles in boundary walls and then bearing sharp left by an old sheepfold. Climb up to the main road opposite Peak View Tea Room.

**3** The firm grassy path away to your left leads into

# Cumberland Clough

the Goyt Valley and the ruins of Errwood Hall (*see* Walk 7).

**H** Cross the stile and road with great care. Walk up the tea room drive and turn right at the finger post to follow a grassy moorland track.

**I** Bear left on reaching the A537 and follow the road back to the Cat and Fiddle Inn.

Cat & Fiddle, the second highest pub in England

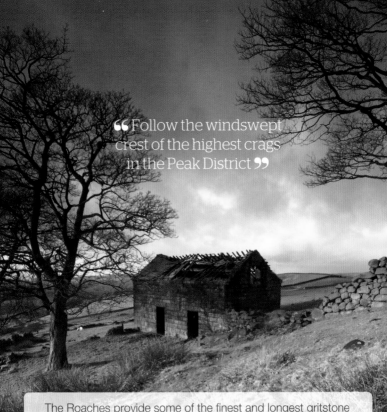

> **"Follow the windswept crest of the highest crags in the Peak District "**

The Roaches provide some of the finest and longest gritstone climbs in the Peak District. This is where many of the famous local climbers such as Joe Brown and Don Whillans first developed their skills. Routes of every standard can be found on these crags and climbers will be seen almost every day of the year attempting what might seem impossibly acrobatic moves.

French monks established their Dieulacresse Abbey close by; below what is now Tittesworth Reservoir. They, with what in hindsight sounds like a lack of imagination, gave the crags the name 'Rocher' which is French for 'rock'. The name changed to Roaches at a later date but lingers in the old form at Roche Grange.

Today the moors and the Roaches themselves are owned by the Peak Park Planning Board. In buying the Roaches Estate, the Board have opened up access to the rocks for climbers and also established a number of concessionary footpaths over the moors, several of which are used to advantage on this walk.

# The Roaches

## Route instructions

**A** Roadside parking is limited below the Roaches. Take care to park where it will not restrict other road users and go through a wicket gate, following the broad track. Aim towards the low col between the Roaches and Hen Cloud.

**B** Turn left and follow the boundary of Rockhall Cottage, towards the lower tier of crags.

**1** Rockhall Cottage. As this building is used as a climbers' club hut, please do not attempt to climb the perimeter wall.

**C** Climb a series of semi natural steps through a gap in the rocks, and above the upper tier of the Roaches. Turn left along their crest.

**2** Viewpoint. The dramatic peak of Hen Cloud is to the southeast. Beyond, the North Staffordshire Plain stretches into the distance.

**3** Doxey Pool. This little pool does not appear to have either an inlet or outlet. It is supposed to be the home of a mermaid.

**4** Viewpoint. Shutlingsloe, Cheshire's 'Matterhorn', rises above the Dane Valley and the hills of North Wales can often be seen in hazy outline across the Cheshire Plain. Approximately due west, a hill known as The Cloud can be seen above Rudyard Lake.

## Plan your walk

**DISTANCE:** 7 miles (11.3km)

**TIME:** 3½ hours

**START/END:** SK004621

**TERRAIN:** Strenuous; one 608ft (185m) climb

**MAPS:**
OS Explorer OL 24;
OS Landranger 119

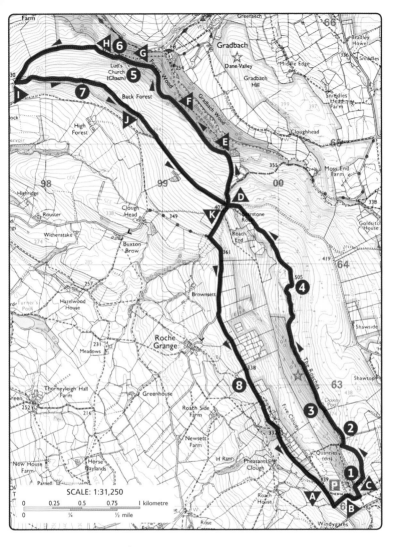

**D** Cross the road and turn right down an access track for about 50yds (46m). Turn left through a narrow stile and then go downhill to the right over the rough moor, following the direction of yellow waymark arrows and the boundary wall.

**E** Turn left, away from the more distinct path and skirt the upper edge of the pine wood.

# The Roaches

▶ Go to the left on a concessionary path but keep walking ahead at a sign-posted junction. Cross an area of scrub covered moor.

**5** Lud's Church. It is said that the cave was a refuge for Walter de Ludank, a follower of Wycliffe who held dissenting services here in the 14th century. A more ancient legend connects it with the Green Chapel of the medieval poem 'Sir Gawain and the Green Knight'. If this is correct, then it was on this spot that King Arthur's champion met and fought the green knight.

▶ Climb down the steps into Lud's Church. Be careful, as the steps and rocks can be slippery when wet. Bear left on leaving the cave.

**6** Viewpoint. Castle Cliff Rocks make an ideal picnic spot above the Upper Dane.

▶ Follow a level sandy path through ancient woodland.

▶ Do not go through the gate but turn left to follow the concessionary path signposted to Roach End. Climb along the crest of the moorland escarpment.

**7** Viewpoint. The nearby valley is the Dane.

▶ In the shallow col, walk ahead at a path junction.

▶ Turn right and follow the gated moorland road along the foot of the Roaches, back to the car park.

**8** At one time there were many small farms in this area. Their owners eked out a bare living by mining coal in shallow pits on the moors. Many of the small holdings still exist, with the present day owners working in nearby towns and farming in their spare time.

Lud's Church

> **Tranquil dales and natural flower gardens lead the walker through an idyllic landscape**

Many people believe these to be the finest dales in the Peak. The quiet waters of the Wye flow through aptly-named Water-cum-Jolly, contrasting well with the mysterious ravine of Cressbrook Dale. Tideswell Dale provides further interest with its colourful wild flowers every summer.

# Tideswell, Miller's & Cressbrook Dales

Tideswell Dale

## Route instructions

**Plan your walk**

**DISTANCE:** 7½ miles
(12km)

**TIME:** 3¾ hours

**START/END:** SK153741

**TERRAIN:** Moderate;
one 400ft (122m) climb

**MAPS:**
OS Explorer OL 24;
OS Landranger 119

**A** The walk starts from the car park at the Tideswell Dale picnic site. Follow a well-defined path down the dale.

**1** Viewpoint. An old quarry is above and to the left. It was exploited for brown dolerite, a form of basalt left by prehistoric volcanic activity. The steep limestone ramparts of Raven's Tor are ahead.

**B** Turn left along the macadamed road through the settlement and mill yard of Litton Mill.

**2** Litton Mill. This old textile mill has a notorious history. It was founded in 1782, and was run on the virtual slave labour of orphans and other unfortunates who fell into the 'care' of the 'Guardians of the Poor'. Housed in crowded barracks which can still be seen beyond the mill, they worked a 15 hour, six day week, and were fed on gruel and thin broth augmented by oatcakes and black treacle. The mill has recently been converted into modern apartments.

**C** Go through the mill yard, bear right and follow the concessionary path through the wooded confines of Miller's Dale. Walk along the riverside path.

**3** Viewpoint. The partly flooded section of the dale and its smooth walled limestone crags topped by steep grassy upper slopes,

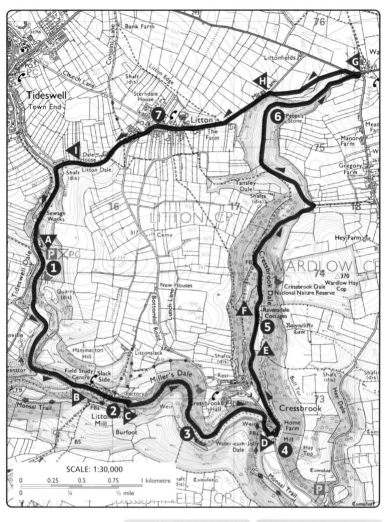

is known by the delightful name of Water-cum-Jolly Dale.

▶ Go through the mill yard at Cressbrook Mill to join the road. Turn left and, within the space of a few yards, go right at a fork in the road.

**4** Cressbrook Mill. This building is of considerable architectural merit but has ceased to produce textiles. Once powered by water, it was built originally for Richard Arkwright, father of the mechanised factory system. This mill has also

# Tideswell, Miller's & Cressbrook Dales

been converted into apartments.

**E** Take the wooded lane on the right to Ravenside Cottages.

**5** Viewpoint. Watercress still grows in Cressbrook's stream and the wooded dale is now a nature reserve. Ravencliffe Cave, in the crags on the eastern rim, was the home of some of our prehistoric forebears.

**F** Follow the signposted path on the left of the row of cottages. Walk along the wooded dale and out into its rocky, treeless upper reaches.

**6** Peter's Stone. This curious detached crag is reputed to be haunted by the last man to hang from a gibbet on its summit.

**G** Go past a stone barn and left of a cottage to join the road. Turn left for 100yds (91m), then left again through a narrow stone stile. Follow the field path uphill to reach the Litton road.

**H** Turn left at the road and follow it through Litton village.

**7** Litton Village. Limestone cottages front a series of little greens and an ancient cross stands on one of them. They dress the Litton wells towards the end of June.

**I** Walk by road down Litton Dale and turn left along the Tideswell Dale road to return to the starting point.

Above Tideswell Dale

> ❝Limestone uplands contrast attractively with the sylvan beauty of Cressbrook Dale❞

The walk explores and compares the scenery of the uplands and wooded dales around Cressbrook, a dale which is so special that it has been designated a nature reserve. Many interesting fossils can be found and admired in the limestone rocks along with the flowers of Cressbrook Dale. Links with the now abandoned industries of the area can be seen. On the higher ground, chert – a particularly hard form of limestone used in pottery making – was quarried below Longstone Edge. Water-powered and elegant Georgian Cressbrook Mill in the dale bottom was founded by Richard Arkwright and was one of the earliest textile mills in the area.

Parking is available at the Monsal Head car park, behind the Monsal Head Hotel.

# Cressbrook Dale

Peter's Stone from
Upper Cressbrook Dale

## Route instructions

**A** Walk down the Longstone road as far as the Packhorse Inn.

**B** Turn left at the signpost to Chertpit Lane and Wardlow. Cross a series of small meadows using stiles in their boundaries.

**C** Turn right along the walled lane as far as the picnic site.

**1** Rough ground at the left-hand side of the track indicates the site of an abandoned chert quarry. Chert is similar to the flint which occurs in the south of England, and both materials were used in the production of bone china.

**D** Turn left along a track at the picnic site and climb the rough wooded hillside.

**E** Where the track ends, climb over a stile and follow the wall to your right for about 100yds (90m), then bear left downhill, crossing field boundaries by their stiles.

**2** Heather is colonizing the moor on the right, a rarity on the limestone uplands of the White Peak. Humps and hollows to your left are the remains of trial holes and small pits left by lead miners.

**F** Turn right at the road. Continue ahead at the crossroads and go downhill into Wardlow.

**3** Half-right and in the middle distance, Eyam Edge

Plan your walk

**DISTANCE:** 6 miles (9.5km)

**TIME:** 3 hours

**START/END:** SK185715

**TERRAIN:** Moderate

**MAPS:**
OS Explorer OL 24;
OS Landranger 119

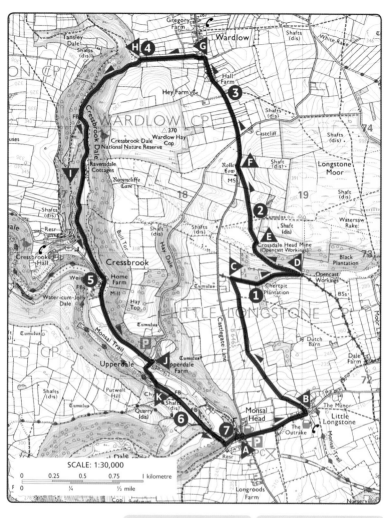

marks the start of the Dark Peak. Kinder Scout, the highest point of Derbyshire can be seen beyond the plume of smoke issuing from the Hope Valley cement works. Closer to hand is the linear village of Wardlow, a feature of the White Peak where farms using a common water supply are infilled by attractive stone cottages.

Turn left along a walled grassy path marked to Ravendale.

**4** Cressbrook Dale is below, as pretty as its name suggests. Designated as a

# Cressbrook Dale

National Nature Reserve, many rare and semi-alpine plants bloom on its dry, grassy heights or in the shady woodland depths. Lily-of-the-valley, primroses, orchids, cowslips, and wood anemones can be found in spring and early summer.

The cave in Ravencliffe, high on the left along the lip of the dale, once yielded gold objects left by the earliest people to live in the Peak District. Please note that there is no public access to the cave.

**H▶** Climb the stile and bear left down the narrow path into the wooded dale.

**I▶** Go past a group of cottages and turn left along the road. Then turn left along the valley road again on reaching the mill.

**5** Cressbrook Mill, a former textile mill, dates from 1815, and replaced one built in 1779 by Richard Arkwright. Water-cum-Jolly Dale, upstream of the mill, provided its water power.

**J▶** Turn right at Upperdale Farm. Cross the river and climb up to the Monsal Trail.

**K▶** Go under a bridge, bear left and then right along the trail. Cross the viaduct and climb to the left, up the wooded slope to Monsal Head.

**6** Monsal Trail. The walkers' and cyclists' route, the Monsal Trail, follows part of the old Midland Railway from Bakewell to Miller's Dale. The line, built at the height of the railway boom of the mid-19th century, was planned to connect London and Manchester by following the Derwent Valley north from Derby. The intended route was along the valley as far as Hathersage where it would join the Sheffield to Manchester line. When it reached Rowsley, the then Duke of Devonshire realized the implications, and forbad progress through Chatsworth. For several years, the line finished at Rowsley before the Monsal line could be built.

The tunnels are illuminated, making it possible to walk all the way from Bakewell to beyond Miller's Dale.

**7** At Monsal Head the dale makes an almost right-angled turn beneath the viaduct. On your left is a group of rocks, called Hob House, which was once part of a coral reef. Prehistoric people lived at Fin Cop on the dale's rim high above the outcrop. (No public access).

**66** Here is a stroll across flower-filled meadows followed by a lakeside ramble into a town made famous by its puddings **99**

This walk runs northwards from Bakewell to join the Monsal Trail and returns by way of Ashford in the Water and its nearby lake. Several paths used on the walk were originally packhorse ways, themselves based on some of the oldest tracks in the Peak. Monday is Bakewell's market day when parking can be a problem.

# Ashford Lake

The walk starts and finishes near this ancient bridge

## Plan your walk

**DISTANCE:** 5½ miles (9km)

**TIME:** 2¾ hours

**START/END:** SK217685

**TERRAIN:** Easy

**MAPS:**
OS Explorer OL 24;
OS Landranger 119

## Route instructions

**A** Follow the main road north-west from the town centre past the fire station. Turn right over the pack-horse bridge.

**1** Holme packhorse bridge was built in 1664.

**B** Take the rough surfaced lane ahead and walk uphill past the old chert mine.

**C** Go through a metal gate and follow the path through open fields.

**2** Look back on Bakewell sheltering in its sunny hollow.

**3** Look across Hassop Park to Longstone Edge. The roadside cottage below was a tollhouse.

**D** Turn left along the Monsal Trail.

**4** The Monsal Trail follows part of the Midland Railway that ran from London to Manchester.

**E** At a signpost, turn right from the trail. Go down the embankment and turn right along a path towards the road. Turn right again and go under the bridge. Cross the road junction and walk up the farm lane opposite.

**F** Follow the footpath sign to the left, then right around Churchdale Hall.

**G** Cross a stile then go downhill to the road, and turn left.

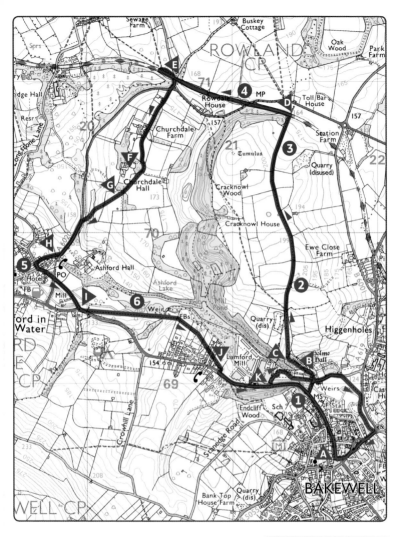

**H** Turn right down a path at the first cottages in Ashford in the Water. Go to the left through the village. Cross the A6020 and go down the side road to cross the abandoned bridge.

**5** Divert through Ashford to visit Sheepwash Bridge at the far end of the main street. There are two pubs and restaurants.

**I** Turn left along the main road for about 80yds (73m),

# Ashford Lake

then left through a kissing gate. Follow the path above the riverbank.

**6** Ashford Lake once powered mills in Bakewell.

▶ Go through a housing estate, across a narrow field to the road, and turn left.

**K** ▶ At the mill, turn left over the bridge and then bear right through the car park. Follow the road past the turning to the packhorse bridge and turn right at a kissing gate. Follow the path across the water meadows back to Bakewell.

Ashford Church

Walkers are free to roam over much of the parkland and woods surrounding Chatsworth; this walk takes advantage of that opportunity. Starting by first moving away from Chatsworth Park, the walk visits Beeley. Its houses are built of gritstone with a warm, grey hue and the church seems slightly aloof from the rest of the village. Every spring, its graveyard is a mass of wild daffodils.

Beyond Beeley, the route climbs inappropriately named Hell Bank Plantation to reach the open space of Beeley Moor. It then descends, only to climb again by a concessionary path into sheltering game forests to the east of Chatsworth House.

66 Enjoy the freedom of the moors and parkland laid out by Capability Brown and Joseph Paxton 99

# Chatsworth

**The Emperor Fountain, Chatsworth**

## Plan your walk

**DISTANCE:** 6 miles (9.6km)

**TIME:** 3 hours

**START/END:** SK259683

**TERRAIN:** Moderate; one 600ft (183m) climb

**MAPS:**
OS Explorer OL 24;
OS Landranger 119

## Route instructions

**A** Park at Calton Lees, south of Chatsworth Park, and walk down to the narrow bridge. Cross and turn right through the metal kissing gate. Follow the field path.

**B** Leave the field by another kissing gate. Cross the road and go into Beeley village. Follow the narrow road at the side of Beeley Brook.

**C** Where the road turns right, walk ahead on a grassy path. Climb a stile on the right and follow a path uphill into forest.

**D** Bear right, still in the forest, and cross the stream above a small waterfall.

**E** Climb a stile in the wall

and turn left, downhill on a rough lane until it bears left.

**F** Cross the stone-stepped stile and follow a moorland track curving first left and then right.

**1** Viewpoint. The view is downward across the pine forest of Hell Bank Plantation and then by way of Beeley to the Derwent Valley. The Wye Valley and limestone uplands are beyond.

**G** Follow the level track and then cross a high stone stile to join a wide forest track, bearing first right then left.

**2** Swiss Cottage (private). This quaint Victorian folly lies across Swiss Lake. Pheasants bred in the

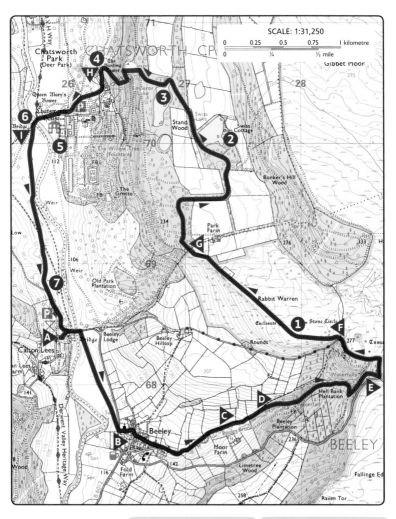

surrounding forest often give themselves away by their raucous rattle. More gentle sounds come from the smaller woodland birds of the area.

**3** Emperor Lake. The lake provides the natural pressure to lift water 290ft (88m) high in the Emperor Fountain, one of Chatsworth's many features. This spectacular fountain can be seen over a considerable distance when fully operational. It was made to impress Tsar Nicholas I of Russia who, unfortunately, never came to see it.

# Chatsworth

**4** The Elizabethan Hunting Tower was built to enable the ladies of Chatsworth to watch the hunt in the parkland below. Chatsworth spreads in all its glory. The present house, home of the Dukes of Devonshire, was built in the 18th century in the Palladian style. Capability Brown landscaped the park and gardens but the present gardens were designed by Sir Joseph Paxton (1803-1865) for the sixth Duke.

Edensor (pronounced 'Ensor') is beyond the small hill across the river from the Hall. Until 1838, the village stood closer to the Hall, but the sixth Duke decided to have the whole village moved as he felt it spoiled his view.

▶ Turn left at a wooden electricity pole and walk past the Hunting Tower. Go down a series of narrow stone steps. Cross a forest road, then right at the next. Keep to the left of the children's farm and walk past the main entrance to Chatsworth House.

**5** The Queen Mary's Bower. The moated tower, a little to the right of the bridge is all that remains of the Elizabethan Chatsworth built by Bess of Hardwick.

Mary Queen of Scots, in her sad and long captivity, was imprisoned at Chatsworth in the care of the Earl of Shrewsbury, husband of Bess. The Bower is said to have been one of her favourite haunts. It was Bess's grandson who became the first Duke of Devonshire by helping William III to gain the throne. The title should be 'Derbyshire' but, due to there already being a Derby title, it was 'Devonshire'.

**6** Viewpoint. This is the most famous view of the house. You can tell, by the number of young trees, that the park is constantly being updated. This is to preserve the scene laid out by Capability Brown two hundred years ago.

▶ Follow the drive over the bridge away from Chatsworth House. Turn left on the far side and follow a pathless route back to the car park. Keep close to the river for the best views.

**7** The Old Mill. This was the estate mill, last used in 1950 for grinding corn. Severely damaged by a storm in 1962, the romantic ruin has been preserved as part of the park. Remnants of the water wheel and grinding machinery can still be seen inside the otherwise empty shell.

**66** Two delightfully contrasting
dales are here linked
by open fields **99**

The walk begins in Youlgreave – a village which is linked, albeit historically, with lead mining. Some of the oldest village buildings are still farms and are firmly part of the village structure despite modern development. Officially, Youlgreave is usually spelt with an 'e' but the locals prefer it as Youlgrave.

Below the village, in quiet Bradford Dale, trout pools originally provided water to power both corn and lead mills. Climbing out of the dale, the walk follows a series of grassy paths across the lush pastures of Calling Low Farm. Through the trees, one of the finest views across the limestone plateau opens up. Dropping quickly into Cales Dale, the path then leads through the sylvan tranquility of Lathkill Dale, a dale which was once the scene of intensive mining activity but is now a completely natural valley.

# Youlgreave & Lathkill Dale

**walk**

**15**

**Lathkill Dale from above Ricklon Dale**

## Route instructions

**A** Car parking can usually be found at either end of the village. The walk starts in the main street, away from the church.

**1** Opposite the youth hostel, there is a large circular stone water tank. On the dry limestone plateau, obtaining water has been a problem which Youlgreave overcame by bringing it across Bradford Dale from nearby Stanton Moor.

**B** Turn left down Holywell Lane, going past the village hall to reach Bradford Dale.

**C** Cross a stone clapper bridge and turn right to follow the riverside path upstream past a series of trout pools.

**D** Cross the stream by a broad stone bridge on the right and then go left uphill past a ruined mill. Walk beneath trees as far as the road, then right.

**2** Middleton-by-Youlgreave stands at the head of Bradford Dale. You can reach it from stage **D** of the route by turning left instead of right at the main road.

**E** Follow the road to the second bend and go left through a stone squeezer stile at the side of a white gate. Cross the field and reach the upper road by a step stile. Ignore the path opposite but turn left to follow the road for about 50yds (46m).

## Plan your walk

**DISTANCE:** 8 miles (12.9km)

**TIME:** 4 hours

**START/END:** SK211643

**TERRAIN:** Moderate

**MAPS:**
OS Explorer OL 24;
OS Landranger 119

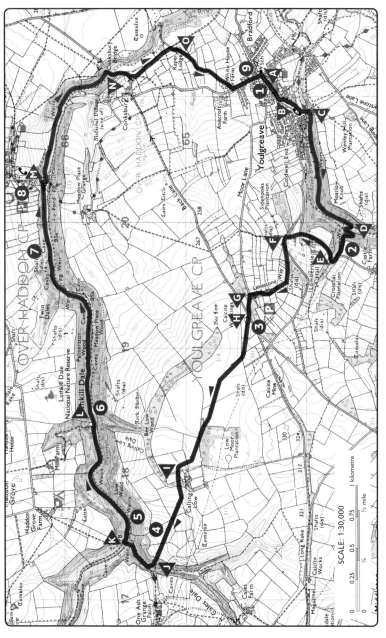

# Youlgreave & Lathkill Dale

**F** Climb the stile on the right and follow a field path uphill as far as the Moor Lane picnic site.

**G** Turn left along the road for a few yards and straight on at the junction.

**3** The road crosses a tree lined cutting following the line of Long Rake lead vein. Latterly, the Rake has been worked from the surface to extract fluorspar.

**H** Climb the wall stile on the right and cross a series of grassy fields, following occasional waymark posts.

**I** Keep right, following signs, around Calling Low Farm.

**4** Viewpoint. Lathkill Dale is the wooded ravine to your right and Monyash church spire can be glimpsed in the distance. Directly opposite, across Cales Dale, is One Ash Grange, a prosperous sheep farm, once a monastic penitentiary.

**J** Climb the stile and go steeply down the stepped path into shrubby Cales Dale. Turn right along the dale bottom.

**K** Cross the wooden footbridge and turn right, following the riverside path along Lathkill Dale.

**5** Natural woodland covering the opposite hillside is part of a nature reserve.

**L** Enter private woodland by following a concessionary footpath.

**6** Stone pillars mark the line of a viaduct which carried water across the dale to Mandale Mine.

**7** Mandale was one of the largest lead mines in the locality but only the shell of its pit-head gear now remains.

**8** Over Haddon is to the left, about ½ mile (0.8km) away by the steep side road.

**M** At the end of the wood, go right, then left around the boundary of a large house. Follow the path along the river bank.

**N** On reaching the road, turn right over Conksbury Bridge for about 120yds (110m), then left through a squeezer stile on to a field path.

**O** Follow the field path. Turn right at a narrow lane, past Raper Lodge to reach Youlgreave.

**9** Youlgreave's historic church is well worth a visit. Look inside at the radiant colours of the east window.

> **❝** Enjoy this little known corner of the White Peak dales' landscape **❞**

Two little-known White Peak dales are explored on this walk from the secluded village of Middleton-by-Youlgreave. The first, Bradford Dale, has a river but Long Dale is dry. Between them, high limestone pastures are crossed along the way, offering wide-ranging views over the surrounding countryside.

Middleton might seem a sleepy place today, but it has seen plenty of activity down the centuries. It once had a castle although nothing remains apart from a mound and, during the English Civil War, a bloody skirmish took place nearby.

Sculptures passed along the way mark Middleton's parish boundary. Known locally as 'Sites of Interest', they were erected as a Millennium project. No two are alike.

# Middleton & Long Dale

**Bradford Dale**

## Route instructions

### Plan your walk

**A** Go down the lane opposite the playground into Bradford Dale, and turn right.

**B** Cross the footbridge and climb the slope, then down again to recross the stream, by a stone-slab bridge. Cross the next fields by using stiles in their walls.

**1** A partly overgrown pond in the dale bottom is the upper of a series of small reservoirs. Now the home of trout, the river was dammed creating water power to drive a lead-crushing mill at Alport lower down the dale.

**C** Go over the narrow lane to follow a tiny brook upstream. Where it bends to your left, continue ahead,

to the right, above a wooded ravine.

**2** The underlying strata on your side of the stream dip sharply towards Rowlow Brook. Rocks on the far side of the brook have been worn into overhangs by water action, partly by the stream, but mostly by floodwater at the end of the Ice Age.

**D** Turn left along the road.

**E** Where the road bends sharply left, continue ahead and uphill, along the sunken track and then through open fields.

**3** Look back along the way you have come. Bradford Dale points towards the

**DISTANCE:** 6 miles (9.5km)

**TIME:** 3 hours

**START/END:** SK195632

**TERRAIN:** Moderate

**MAPS:**
OS Explorer OL 24;
OS Landranger 119

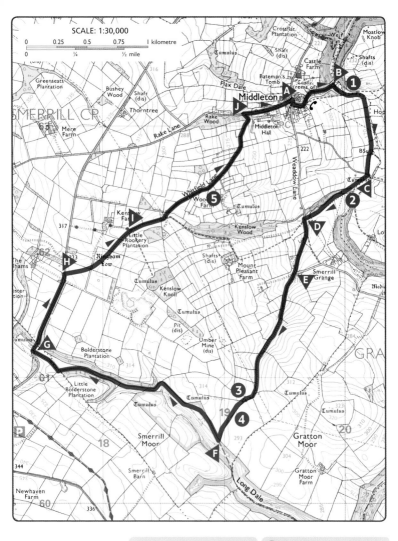

prominent square tower of Youlgreave Church. Beyond and across the deep trough of the Derwent Valley, wooded slopes above Chatsworth climb towards heather-clad Beeley Moor, a purple riot every summer.

**4** Almost secretive, Long Dale is below, a completely dry dale supporting short but succulent grazing. On the opposite hillside are humps and hollows, the remains of trial holes from a time when the White

# Middleton & Long Dale

Peak yielded its hoard of lead ore. Over to the left and on the highest point of the skyline, a lonely clump of trees marks the site of Minninglow, the largest and most important tumulus in the Peak. In May and June look for the tiny, pansy-like flower known locally as 'Heart's ease'; Viola tricolor is usually blue but it is sometimes yellow in the limestone dales of the Peak District.

**F** Drop steeply into Long Dale. Turn right along the dale bottom. Bear left at the first clump of trees. Cross a stile and go to the right along a narrow field between two sets of woodland. Go through an old gateway and follow the grassy track parallel to the field.

**G** Climb up to the road and turn right along it for a little under ½ mile (800m).

**H** Go over a stone stile on the right and cross five fields, using stiles to find the route.

**I** Turn right along the farm lane. Where it forks, beyond a large sycamore, bear left along a walled lane.

**5** Bradford Dale reappears below and leads the eye towards the Derwent's heather moors. Land on your left and right is based on limestone all the way to Elton, the former mining village on the far right. The opposite, or southern, side of Bradford Dale is mostly gritstone as indicated by a proliferation of trees which grow best on the moister and acidic soils based on a foundation of gritstone.

**J** Turn right at the road and walk downhill into Middleton.

Bradford Dale

**❝ Here is a walk around the dales leading from an ancient market place ❞**

Hartington has always been a busy village. Ancient Britons are believed to have fought Roman legionaries on nearby Hartington Moor. The village is mentioned in the Domesday Book as 'Hortedun' and had a market as long ago as the 13th century. Its church dates from the 14th century.

Many famous people have either lived or spent part of their lives around Hartington. Literary giants and philosophers, such as Dr Johnson, Byron and Mark Twain, came to admire the beauties of Dovedale. Without doubt, the most famous was Izaak Walton, author of the 17th-century treatise on fishing: *'The Compleat Angler – The Contemplative Man's Recreation'*. Walton was a friend of Charles Cotton, who lived at Beresford Hall, and the part of *'Compleat Angler'* devoted to Dovedale tells of their adventures together.

Beresford Hall has long since disappeared and there have been no markets in Hartington for many years but the village is a hive of activity with the comings and goings of people from the surrounding farms and visitors who use it as a base to explore the Dove and its byways.

# Hartington & its Dales

St Giles Church, Hartington

## Route instructions

**A** From the village, walk as far as the war memorial and turn right up the steep side road.

**1** Hartington Hall. A Jacobean house that is at least 300 years old. Bonnie Prince Charlie is reputed to have slept here during the abortive march on London which got as far as Derby. The house was owned by the Bateman family, one of whom was knighted by Charles II. Another became Lord Mayor of London. Today, Hartington Hall is a tastefully adapted youth hostel.

**B** Turn right opposite the youth hostel, along the walled track.

**C** At the end of the lane go over a stile and turn half right to cross two fields. Aim towards the clump of trees by the roadside.

**2** Viewpoint. The limestone plateau extends in all directions. The prominent rise to the south west across Dovedale is Ecton Hill, one-time source of valuable copper deposits.

**D** Cross the stile and turn left along the metalled lane as far as the cross roads. Walk ahead on a rough cart track.

**E** Pass a well made stone bam. Leave the walled track at a gate and walk downhill on an open path into Biggin Dale. Turn right and walk along the dale bottom.

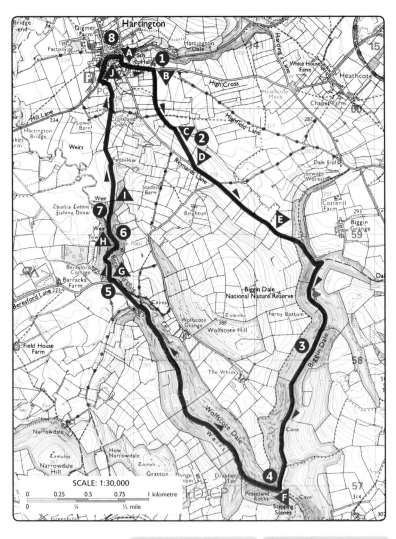

**3** Biggin Dale. Many uncommon plants and flowers grow on its rocky sides. The dale bottom, which only occasionally has surface water, supports blackthorn and other shrubby trees.

**4** Viewpoint. Rocky tors climb the valley sides above the Dove. This area is called Wolfscote Dale, Beresford Dale is nearer Hartington. Only that part downstream below Milldale is truly Dovedale but most

# Hartington & its Dales

people refer to the whole as Dovedale.

**F** Join the main dale and turn right upstream along the east bank of the Dove. The path fills the narrow ledge between the river bank and the loose scree-covered valley side.

**G** Cross the river by the footbridge and turn right, upstream along tree-covered Beresford Dale.

**5** The river is fordable at this point, an important packhorse crossing in olden times.

**H** Cross the footbridge and turn left through woodland along the opposite bank.

**6** Pike Pool. This deep pool was named by Cotton not, as it is said, because pike lived in it, but as a description of the slender spire or 'pike' of rock which reaches out from its depths.

**7** The Fishing Temple. This 'hideaway', shared by Walton and Charles Cotton, is, unfortunately, on private land and only its roof can be glimpsed through the trees. They sat here and contemplated their fishing exploits beneath a doorway marked 'Piscatoribus Sacrum 1674'. Their initials entwined in stone, mark their friendship down the

centuries. Beresford Hall stood further back behind the wooded river bank. Leaving Dovedale, we can understand Walton's parting description of the River Dove as the finest river he ever saw and the most full of fish.

**I** Climb away from the river. Leave the wooded area at a narrow iron gate. Cross a series of fields using the stiles in their boundary walls.

**J** Turn right at the road to return to the centre of Hartington.

**8** Hartington is grouped around its duck pond in the market square. The village has a couple of pubs and several cafés and shops. Locally made cheese is sold in the shop just off the old market square. The Parish Church of St. Giles is well worth a visit for its mediaeval relics and attractive windows.

> **66** The walk follows upland paths around this popular dale to reach a bridge once crossed by mail coaches **99**

Most visitors arriving at the lower reaches of Dovedale are content with a short stroll beyond the stepping stones at the mouth of the dale. Scenically delightful though this may be, it is only a mere hint of the attractions further upstream.

Old prints and photographs show the dale sides almost bare of trees but, in the space of a few decades, the valley became over populated by the rapid spread of ash and sycamore. The National Trust, as owners of Dovedale, have lately been removing much of this new growth from around special features. As a result, natural formations such as Reynard's Cave and the Twelve Apostles' Rocks, can be appreciated as they were in the past. Grass is now regenerating, holding the loose scree and the view of Dovedale is now more open, its beauty preserved for the future.

A gate on a footpath, Dovedale

# Dovedale

Valley of the River Dove, Dovedale

## Plan your walk

**DISTANCE:** 5½ miles (8.8km)

**TIME:** 2¾ hours

**START/END:** SK136509

**TERRAIN:** Moderate; one 538ft (164m) climb

**MAPS:**
OS Explorer OL 24;
OS Landranger 119

## Route instructions

**A** The walk starts in Ilam village. Follow the Thorpe road for a little way beyond the last house and turn left at a signpost. Cross the stile and then bear sharp left, uphill through some bushes.

**1** St. Bertram's Well. St. Bertram or Bertelin brought Christianity to Dovedale in the 7th or 8th century. Legend tells us that he became a hermit following the death of his Irish born wife and his only child who were attacked by a pack of wolves nearby. Heartbroken, he spent the rest of his life in this remote hollow.

**2** Viewpoint. The mock Tudor chimneys of Victorian Ilam Hall can be seen in the valley bottom. Beyond the hall, Hinckley Wood shrouds the steep sides of the lower Manifold Valley.

**B** At the top of the slope, cross two adjoining stiles and follow a pathless course across the next field. Aim for a prominent tree on the crest of the rise.

**C** Go right, then left through two field gates at the side of a stone barn. Follow the track on the right of the shelter belt of trees. Turn right to reach Air Cottage.

**D** Keep to the right of the cottage, and then go left along the valley crest. Join a farm track beyond the cottage.

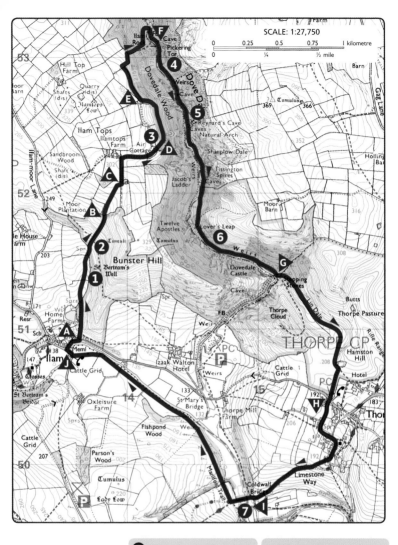

**3** Viewpoint. Air Cottage must have one of the finest views in the Peak District. Set high above Dovedale, you can see Thorpe Cloud on the right, then Lover's Leap, Tissington Spires and Reynard's Cave. The middle and upper dale can be seen curving away to the north as a narrow ravine cleaving its way through the limestone uplands.

**E** Climb a ladder stile by the side of a field gate

# Dovedale

and then immediately turn right over another stile into woodland. Keep left on the well defined steep path which eventually drops into the valley.

▶ Turn right at the path junction at the side of the River Dove. Cross sides by the footbridge below Ilam Rock and follow the riverside path downstream.

**4** Lion Rock at the foot of Pickering Tor is aptly named. Look back upstream for the best view.

**5** Reynard's Cave. Look out for a natural arch high above the path on the left. A cave beyond the arch was used as a hiding place during troubled times following the end of the Roman occupation. Arrow heads and pottery have been found in its recesses.

**6** Lover's Leap. The path climbs above the river by a series of steps to reach this rocky vantage point. Opposite, there are rocky spires known as the Twelve Apostles. Autumn is the best time for this part of the dale because this is when the trees are most colourful. There is no record of any star-crossed lovers jumping from this point but there is a cautionary tale concerning the Irish Dean of Clogher. In 1761 he tried to ride over the rock carrying a young lady companion as a pillion passenger. The horse stumbled on the slippery rocks and all three fell towards the river. The Dean was killed and is buried at Ashbourne. The lady was more fortunate, as she was saved by her long hair which caught in the branches of a tree.

**G** Do not go quite as far as the Stepping Stones, but turn sharp left, uphill and beside a wall. Cross the wide col and go downhill towards Thorpe village.

**H** Go past the public toilets and follow the side lane opposite, bearing left then right past the church. Go downhill on the farm lane.

▶ Cross the wide bridge and then turn right. The path is partly screened by bushes, so keep the river on your right and walk upstream.

**7** Coldwall Bridge is rather incongruous in the rural setting, but it is all that remains of an abandoned turnpike road between Cheadle Staffs and Chesterfield.

▶ Climb up to the road. Turn right to cross the bridge and return to Ilam.

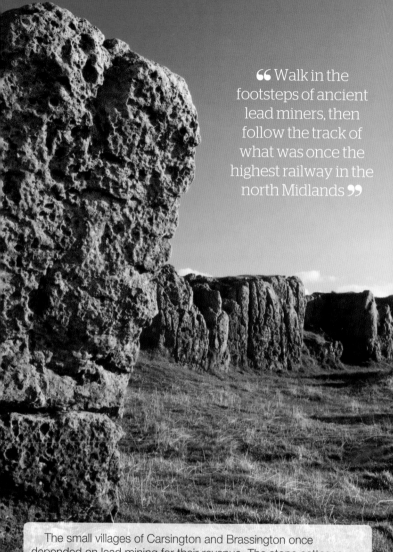

**❝** Walk in the footsteps of ancient lead miners, then follow the track of what was once the highest railway in the north Midlands **❞**

The small villages of Carsington and Brassington once depended on lead mining for their revenue. The stone cottages housed men who scratched a living below ground supplementing their income from part-time farming. Their small holdings are now incorporated within larger farms and the only tangible remains of mining are humps and hollows dotted along the walk.

The walk passes beneath
Harboro' Rocks

# Carsington Pasture

**Carsington Water**

## Route instructions

**Plan your walk**

Halifax · Wakefield · Rochdale · Huddersfield · Oldham · Barnsley · Ashton-under-Lyne · Manchester · Sheffield · Stockport · Macclesfield · Dronfield · Chesterfield · Buxton · Congleton · Leek · Matlock · Newcastle-under-Lyme · Ashbourne · Stoke-on-Trent · Derby · Stone · Uttoxeter

**DISTANCE:** 6¾ miles (10.9km)

**TIME:** 3½ hours

**START/END:** SK251534

**TERRAIN:** Moderate; two climbs of 333ft (101m) and 200ft (61m)

**MAPS:**
OS Explorer OL 24;
OS Landranger 119

**A** Start at the west end of Carsington's village street close to the Miners' Arms pub. Where the road turns sharp left, turn right along a short lane between groups of cottages.

**B** Climb a short flight of steps to reach the field on the right of the last house. There is no continuous footpath but climb the steep field by a zigzag route, aiming for the top right hand corner.

**C** Ignoring a stile, turn left to follow the line of the wall across Carsington Pasture.

**1** King's Chair is a rough hewn seat carved from a limestone block on the opposite side of the wall.

Do not cross as the field is private. The 'chair' looks out over the Henmore Valley and the new Carsington Reservoir.

**D** Cross the road by a couple of stiles and then turn left along the track of the High Peak Trail.

**2** The High Peak Trail follows the track of the Cromford and High Peak Railway.

**3** Harboro' Rocks and similar outcrops are made from dolomitic or magnesian limestone.

**E** Turn right away from the trail between a group of buildings at Longcliffe Wharf, then left along the

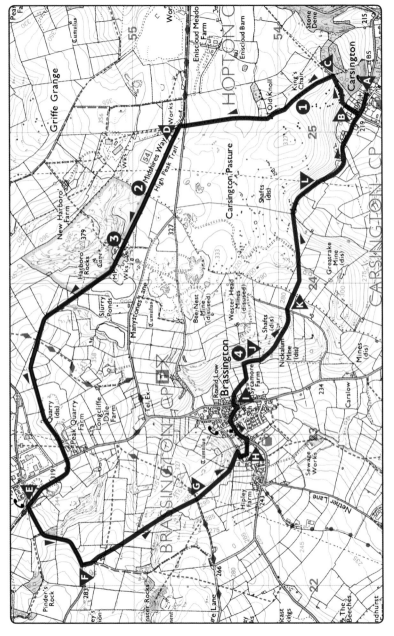

# Carsington Pasture

road. (Stations were known as wharfs on the High Peak Railway.)

**F** Leave the road by a gate on the left. Keep to the left of the prominent barn and cross a series of fields by lining up stiles in field boundary walls.

**G** Cross the head of an access lane and then walk across a rock strewn field to reach Brassington.

**H** Enter the village by crossing a narrow lane and follow a narrow walled path on the right. Turn left through the village and then go past the Gate Inn and the Miners Arms to the second road junction.

**I** Cross the road and keep right through the farmyard opposite. Go through a stile and turn right. Cross three narrow fields, and through stiles in their boundaries. Go left at the last one and climb to the top of the field.

**4** View of Brassington. 'Branzicton' in the Domesday Book.

**J** Turn right through a stile and walk round the grassy hillside.

**K** Cross the lane and climb a couple of fields, aiming to the left of a group of tree shrouded rocks. Go over the brow of the hill.

**L** Follow an improving track down to Carsington.

Wintry sunshine on the High Peak Trail

**66** The walk starts at Smedley's mock castle and then visits a hamlet with tragic links to Mary Queen of Scots **99**

Only the façade of Riber Castle is left standing, currently the subject of a controversial development. Built by John Smedley in the 1850s as a hydropathic establishment, it never succeeded, mainly because it lacked a good water supply! Most of the other buildings in this settlement are Jacobean. From the village, the route uses quiet paths to reach Dethick, and starts high above Matlock but, as an alternative, the walk may be extended from the centre of Matlock by way of Starkholmes and climbing the steep path from the road to the castle.

Parking is limited around Riber, but there is usually space near the road junction.

# Riber & Dethick

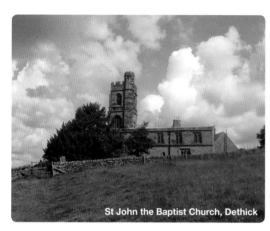

St John the Baptist Church, Dethick

## Route instructions

**A** With your back to Riber Hall, turn right then left at the T-junction for a few yards. Go through the stone stile on the right. Aim across the fields towards a group of cottages and farm buildings.

**1** Most of the older buildings in Riber are Elizabethan or Jacobean.

**B** Go to the left and follow the metalled lane through the farmyard.

**C** Go past a large silo and fork right on to a walled track. Ignore gated side turnings.

**2** The little hill you have just climbed is Bilberry Knoll; clumps of this succulent

fruit grow at the side of the track. Ahead, the wooded Derwent winds its way southwards, and to the left is Crich Stand with its lighthouse memorial to the men of the Sherwood Foresters who died in both world wars. Crich Tramway Museum is in the quarry below the lighthouse.

**D** About 120yds (110m) beyond the corner of a wood on your right, turn left, over a stile, and follow waymarks alongside a holly hedge.

**E** Follow the waymarks to the left, across two fields. Turn right into woodland and go down to stepping stones across a stream. Climb up to the road.

## Plan your walk

**DISTANCE:** 5 miles (8km)

**TIME:** 2½ hours

**START/END:** SK308588

**TERRAIN:** Easy

**MAPS:**
OS Explorer OL 24;
OS Landranger 119

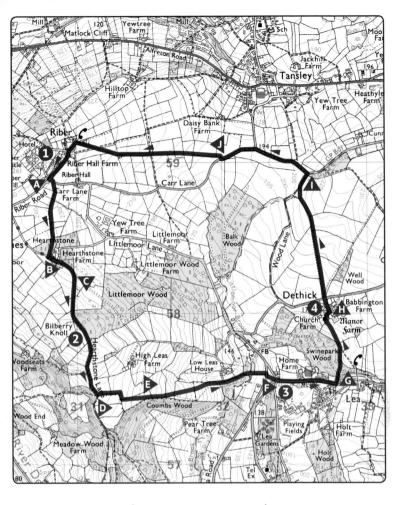

**F** Follow the path between two roads. Go through a stile and ahead into Lea village.

**3** A diversion of about 350yds (320m) to the right leads to Lea Rhododendron Gardens which are highly recommended in early summer.

**G** Turn left at a kissing gate and follow a footpath, signposted to Dethick and Tansley, across the deep, wooded dell. Continue by field path.

**4** The sleepy hamlet of Dethick was the home of the Babbingtons who tried to free Mary Queen of Scots

# Riber & Dethick

during her imprisonment at nearby Wingfield Manor. All that is left of what was once a small settlement are three farms and a church.

**H** Keep to the right of the church, then left through the farmyard. Cross the road and climb a stile. Follow the path beside a stone wall.

**I** Turn right for a little way along a bridleway, then left at the road. At the junction, take the left fork for 300yds (275m).

**J** Where the road drops left, turn right and go through a stile to follow a path directly to Riber.

Matlock from close to Riber Castle

# Photo credits